CONFIGURING LIFECYCLE SERVICES TO MANAGE DYNAMICS AX PROJECTS

BY MURRAY FIFE

ISBN: 1500589756

ISBN-13: 978-1500589752

Preface

What You Need For This Guide

All the examples shown in this blueprint were done with the Microsoft Dynamics AX 2012 virtual machine image that was downloaded from the Microsoft CustomerSource or PartnerSource site. If you don't have your own installation of Microsoft Dynamics AX 2012, you can also use the images found on the Microsoft Learning Download Center or deployed through Lifecycle Services. The following list of software from the virtual image was leveraged within this guide:

* Microsoft Dynamics AX 2012 R3

Even though all the preceding software was used during the development and testing of the recipes in this book, they may also work on earlier versions of the software with minor tweaks and adjustments, and should also work on later versions without any changes.

Errata

Although we have taken every care to ensure the accuracy of our content, mistakes do happen. If you find a mistake in one of our books—maybe a mistake in the text or the code—we would be grateful if you would report this to us. By doing so, you can save other readers from frustration and help us improve subsequent versions of this book. If you find any errata, please report them by emailing editor@dynamicsaxcompanions.com.

Piracy

Piracy of copyright material on the Internet is an ongoing problem across all media. If you come across any illegal copies of our works, in any form, on the Internet, please provide us with the location address or website name immediately so that we can pursue a remedy.

Please contact us at legal@dynamicsaxcompanions.com with a link to the suspected pirated material.

We appreciate your help in protecting our authors, and our ability to bring you valuable content.

Questions

You can contact us at help@dynamicsaxcompanions.com if you are having a problem with any aspect of the book, and we will do our best to address it.

Table Of Contents

9   **INTRODUCTION**

11   **ACCESSING LIFECYCLE SERVICES**

13   Logging Into Lifecycle Services

19   **CONFIGURING LIFECYCLE SERVICES PROJECTS**

21   Creating a New Project

31   Adding Members to the Project Team

41   Creating Additional Project Roles

49   **CREATING BUSINESS PROCESS MODELS**

51   Accessing The Task Recorder

55   Configuring a New Task Recorder Framework

63   Defining Industry Codes

71   Defining Hierarchy Levels for Your Framework

81   Building Your Business Process Framework Structure

95   Creating a Business Process Import Template

103   Importing a Business Process Framework from a Template

115   Configuring The Task Recorder Recording Parameters

123   Recording A Task For a Business Process Element

129   Printing Out The Task Recording Documentation

133   Customizing The Task Recorder Word Template

145   Creating A Data Entry Template From A Task Recording

151   Accessing Task Recording Video

157   Building an Lifecycle Services import Package

165   Importing the Business Process Package into a Lifecycle Services Project

181   Importing Business Process Flows From Other Libraries

191   **ESTIMATING INFRASTRUCTURE REQUIREMENTS THROUGH LIFECYCLE SERVICES**

193   Estimating the User Licenses Using The License Estimator

209   Adding New Departments To The Licensing Estimator

215   Adding Custom Roles To The Licensing Estimator

225   Estimating Hardware Requirements Using The Lifecycle Services Usage Profiler

245   **TRACKING PROJECT DETAILS THROUGH LIFECYCLE SERVICES**

249   Modifying Business Process Flows And Creating Gap Lists

255   Adding Work Estimates to Business Process Flow Steps

261   Creating Business Process Documentation From Process Flows

267   Tracking Issues against the Project

279   Tracking Customizations

287   Attach OneDrive Documents To Business Process Models Within Lifecycle Services

305   **DEPLOYING DYNAMICS AX TEST SYSTEMS THROUGH AZURE**

307   Signing Up For An Azure Account

313   Creating A Dynamics AX Instance On Azure Through Lifecycle Services

342   **SUMMARY**

INTRODUCTION

Lifecycle Services is a new offering from Microsoft that changes everything related to the lifecycle of the Dynamics AX projects - allowing you to track and manage not only the Implementation phase of the Dynamics AX projects, but also manage the Pre-Sales phase as well, incorporating in the prospects into the project.

Because this is a cloud based service, there is no additional software that needs to be loaded in order to give prospects and customers access to all of the information that is available through this service, and also this is a tool that is available for any Customer and Partner that is registered with Microsoft for free making it impossible not to use.

When you roll in the ability to upload Business Process Flow recordings directly from Task Recordings, the ability to have Issue and Customization tracking on-line, and even link with Azure to create test and sandbox environments on the fly with no additional hardware investments, this is a extremely powerful set of tools to take advantage of.

Although we won't be able to show all of the bells and whistles available within this product (because it is literally being enhanced daily) hopefully this book will give you all an idea of the features and functions and also show you how easy it is to use within your own project.

ACCESSING LIFECYCLE SERVICES

The very first step in using Lifecycle Services is to get access to it. In this chapter we will show you how simple this is to do.

Logging Into Lifecycle Services

The very first thing that you need to do is get access to Lifecycle Services. Luckily, if you have a LiveID that is linked to wither CustomerSource or PartnerSource, then you probably have everything that you need in order to access the portal, and since this is a hosted service then there is no software to install in order to access it as well.

Accessing Lifecycle Services

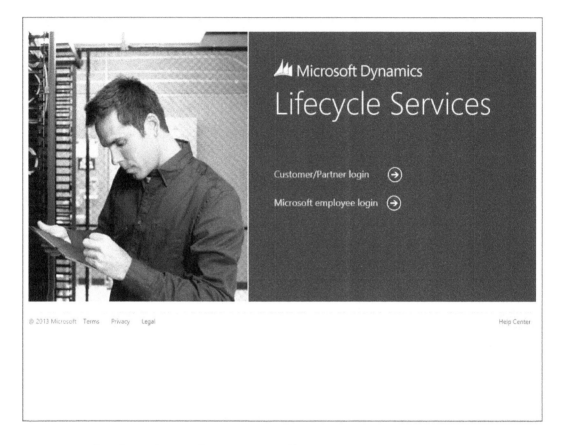

To access **Lifecycle Services** just browser to http://lcs.dynamics.com, and then click on the **Customer/Partner login** button.

Accessing Lifecycle Services

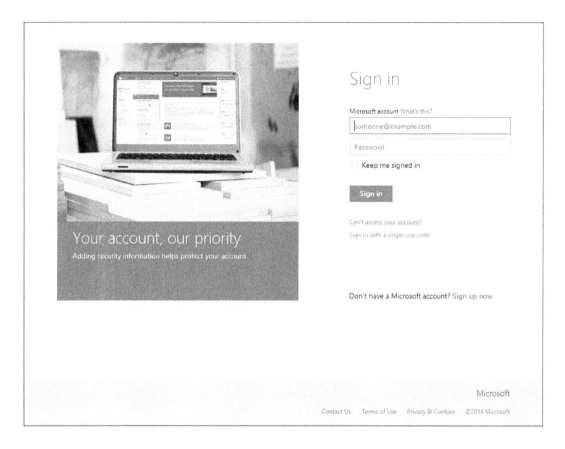

When the **Sign In** page is displayed, log in using your **LiveID** that is associated with your Cusomer/PartnerSource account.

Accessing Lifecycle Services

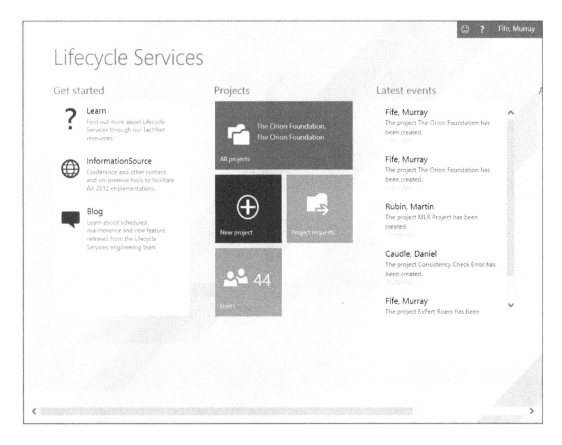

And with a click of the **Sign In** button you will be taken directly to the Lifecycle Services portal.

Now that was easy.

CONFIGURING LIFECYCLE SERVICES PROJECTS

The whole idea of Lifecycle Services is to manage your Dynamics AX Projects, so in this chapter we will show you how to create and configure your **Projects**.

Creating a New Project

Once you have logged into Lifecycle Services, you will probably want to create a new Project that you can start working in.

Creating a New Project

To do this, click on the **New Project** tile within the **Projects** group on the **Lifecycle Services** portal page.

Creating a New Project

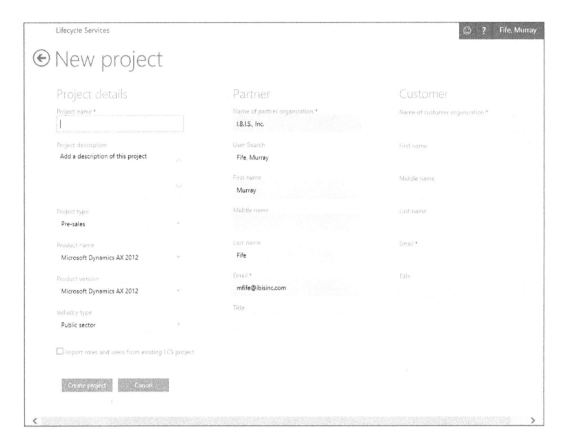

This will take you to a **New Project** setup page.

Creating a New Project

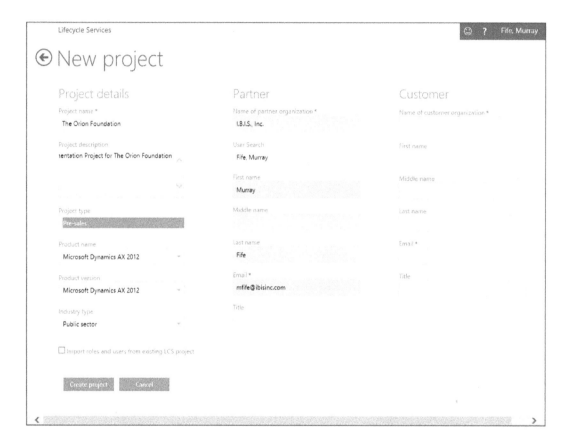

Just enter in the **Project Name** and also a **Project Description**.

Creating a New Project

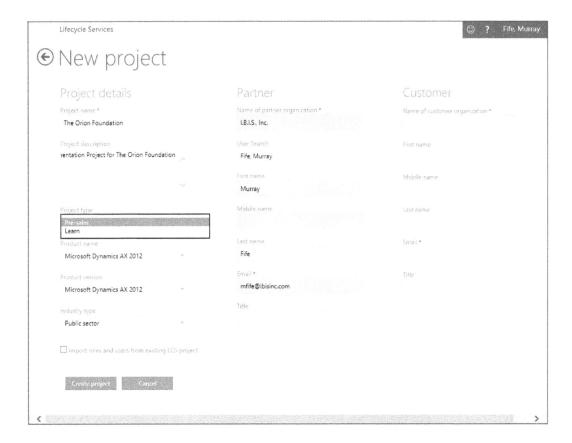

From the **Project Type** selector, choose either the **Pre-Sales** or the **Learn** project type.

Note: If you are a customer, then you will also see different **Project Types** for Implementation etc.

Creating a New Project

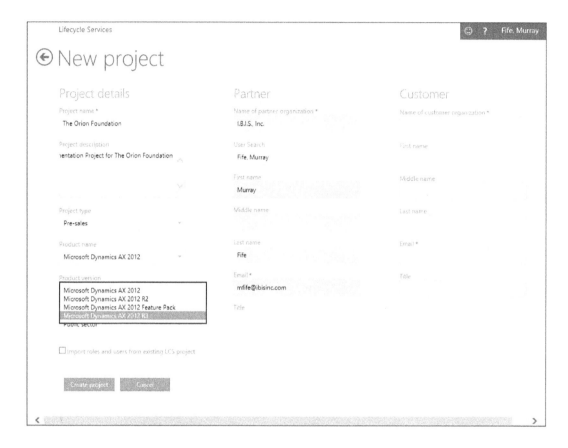

Then from the **Project Version** field, select the version of Dynamics AX that you will be working with within this project.

Creating a New Project

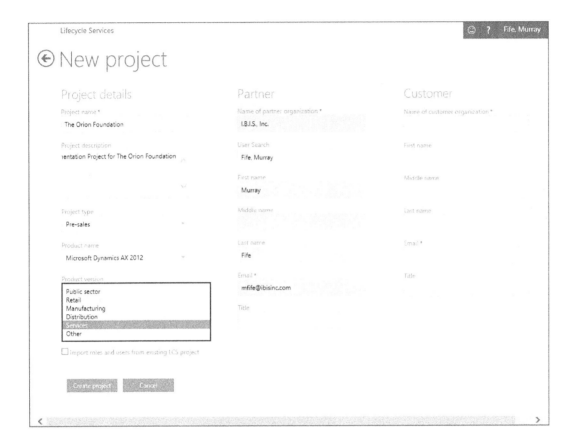

And then select the **Industry Type** that this project is to be tailored to.

Note: This is important, because later on when you select the Business Process Models, if there are tailored models that apply to the industry that you selected, then they will become available.

Creating a New Project

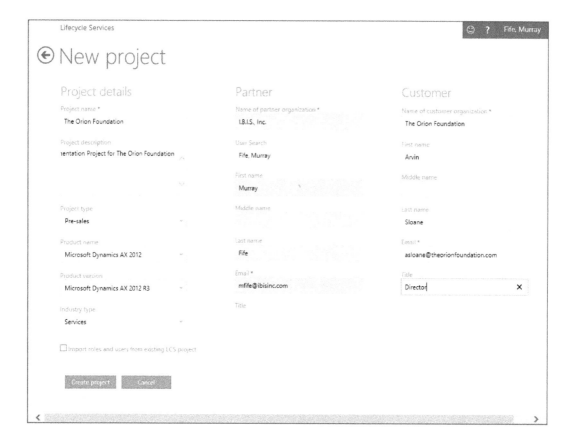

If you selected the **Pre-Sales Project Type** then you will also be asked to enter in the **Customer** details – which will automatically invite that person to the project. If you selected a **Learn** project then this is not required.

When you have filled out the **Project** information then click on the **Create Project** button.

Creating a New Project

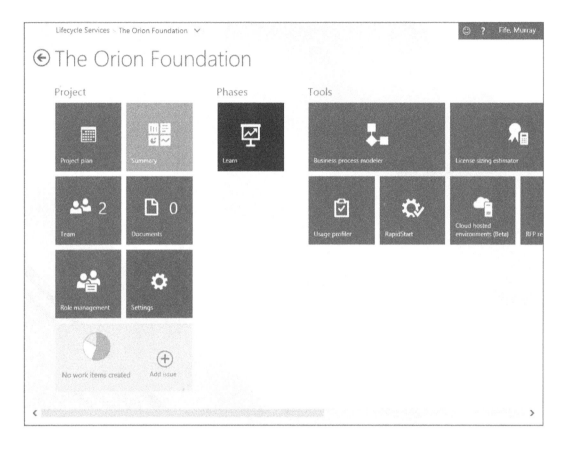

You will then be taken to the **Project** dashboard.

·

Adding Members to the Project Team

Once you have configured your Project, you can start inviting other people to it so that you start collaborating on the project with them.

Adding Members to the Project Team

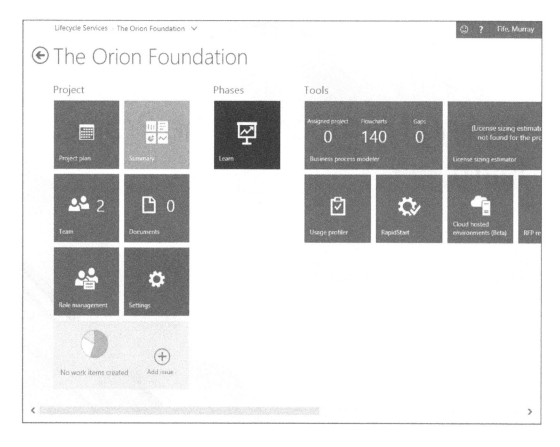

To do this, just click on the **Team** tile within the **Project** group.

Adding Members to the Project Team

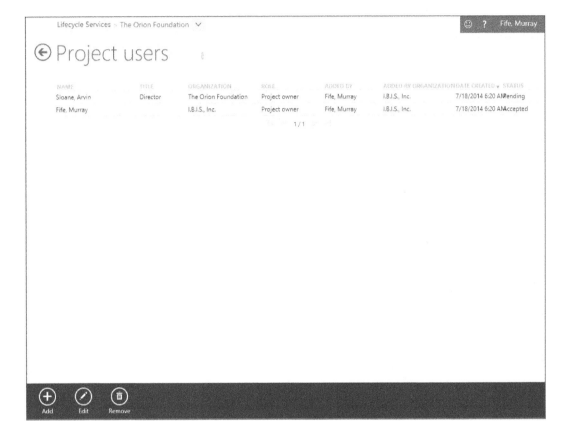

This will open up the **Project Users** page showing all of the current members of the project. To add a new member, just click on the **Add** button in the bottom right of the form.

Adding Members to the Project Team

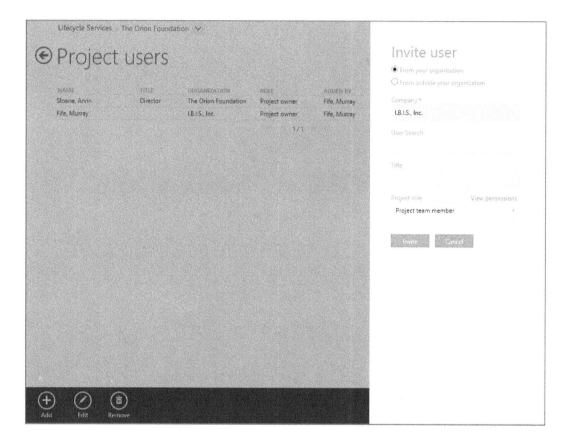

This will open up a **Invite User** panel. If the user is part of your company then you can select the **From Your Organization** radio button and then search for then within your existing users.

Adding Members to the Project Team

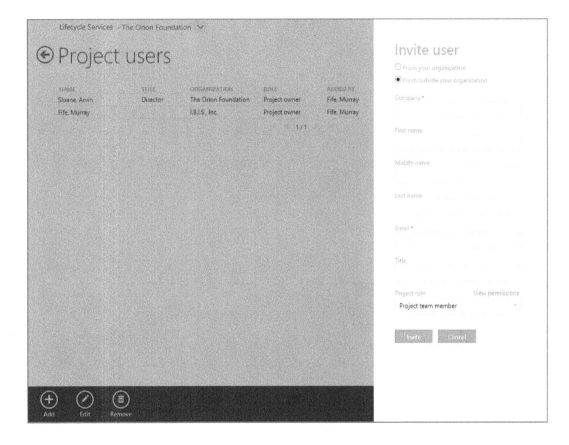

If the user is outside of your organization, then select the **From Outside Your Organization** radio button and you will be able to enter in a freeform user.

Adding Members to the Project Team

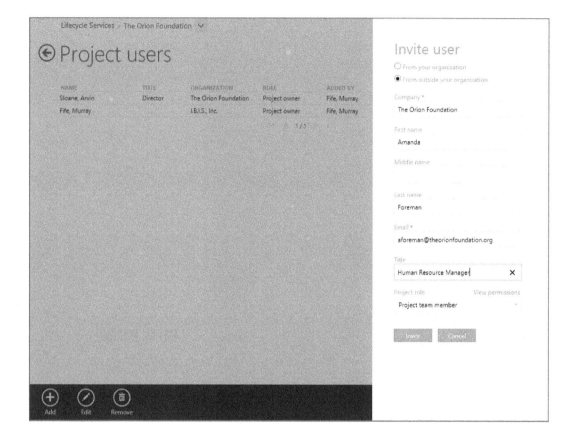

Just enter in the **Company**, **First** and **Last Name**, their **Email** address where you will be sending the invitation to join the project to and then a **Title**.

Then click on the **Invite** button.

Adding Members to the Project Team

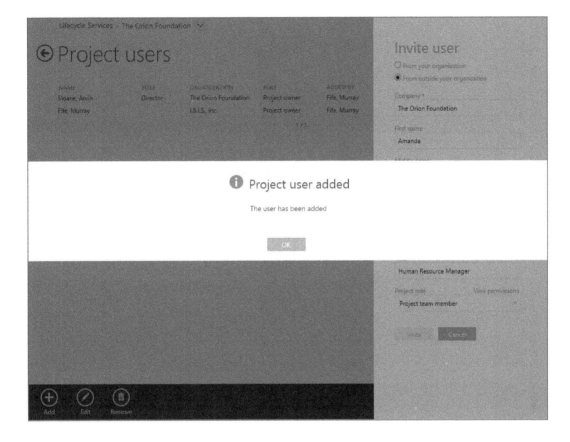

Lifecycle Services will add the user for you and also send out an invitation to them asking them to join the project.

Adding Members to the Project Team

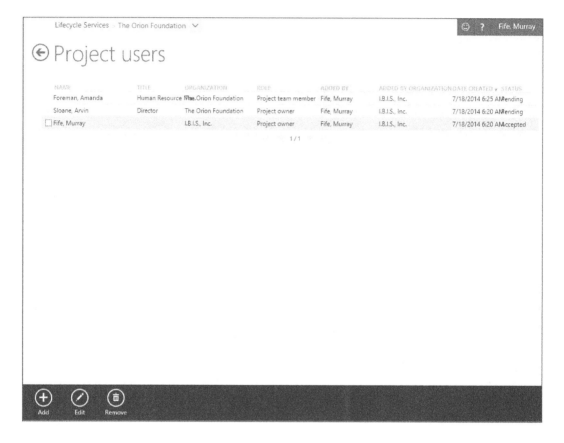

When you return to the **Project Users** page you will see that the user has been added, and given a **Pending** status saying that they have not accepted the invitation yet.

You can keep on adding as many other project members as you like.

Creating Additional Project Roles

There are three default Project Roles that get created with your Lifecycle Services projects, but that does not mean you have to stop there. If you want to create additional custom roles and tweak the security associated with them to give people different access rights then just go right on and do it.

Creating Additional Project Roles

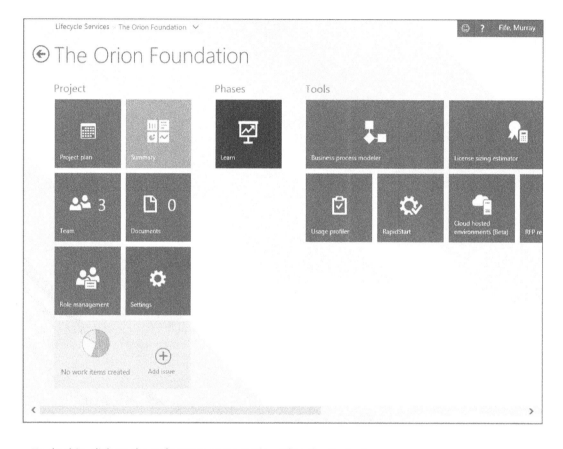

To do this, click on the **Role Management** tile within the **Project** group.

Creating Additional Project Roles

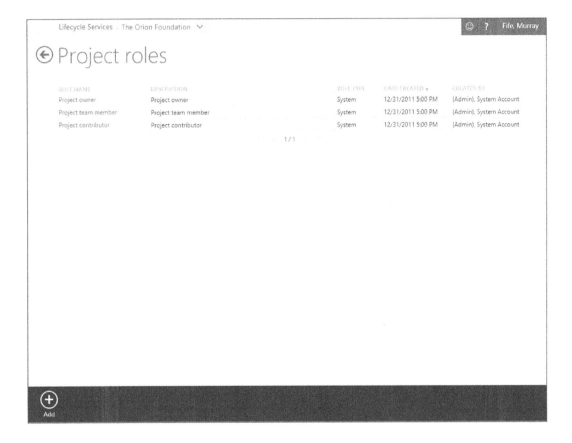

This will open up the **Project Roles** page. To add a new **Project Role,** just click on the **Add** button in the bottom left of the form.

Creating Additional Project Roles

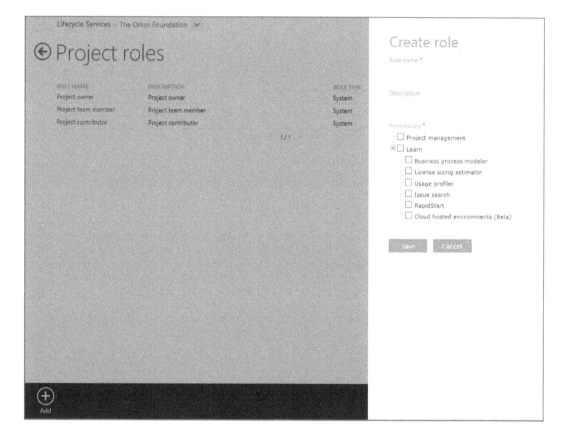

This will open up a **Create Role** panel for you.

Creating Additional Project Roles

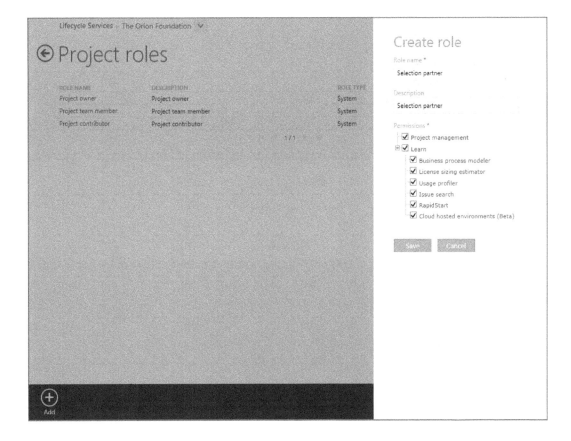

Just enter in the **Role Name**, a **Description**, and then select all of the role **Permissions** that you want to assign to the Project Role.

When you are done, just click the **Save** button.

Creating Additional Project Roles

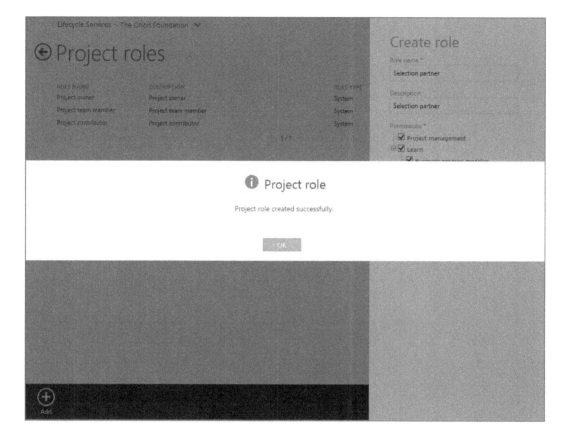

Lifecycle Services will add the Project Role for you and all you need to do now is click the **OK** button.

Creating Additional Project Roles

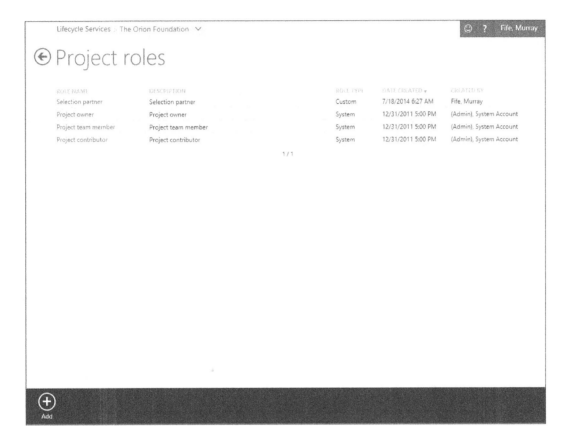

When you return to the **Project Roles** page you will see that the new **Project Role** has been added.

If you want to add more **Project Roles** then just repeat the process.

CREATING BUSINESS PROCESS MODELS

The Task Recorder has always been a useful tool within Dynamics AX, but with the release of Lifecycle Services, it has been upgraded to become even more useful. Now the Task Recorder includes the ability to group your recordings into separate frameworks for different purposes, and also allows you to create a hierarchy structure that you can use to organize your tasks and recordings.

In addition to being able to export your task recordings out to Word etc. for off-line documentation, it also allows you to package up all of the business process structures and import them into Lifecycle Services to use them for managing your project and also collaborating with customers and partners. All of the task recordings are converted to process flow charts within Lifecycle Services to that you can adjust the standard business processes to match your requirements, and also all of the task recordings are viewable as live videos making them a centralized documentation tool for all the key business areas during and after the implementation.

In this chapter we will show how you can set up and configure the business processes within the Task Recorder, create task recordings, and then import the business processes into Lifecycle Services to make them available through via the cloud.

Accessing The Task Recorder

Before we start we need find the **Task Recorder**. Fortunately that's not hard to do since it is part of the standard set of tools that are available within the Dynamics AX client.

In this example we will show how to open up the **Task Recorder**.

Accessing The Task Recorder

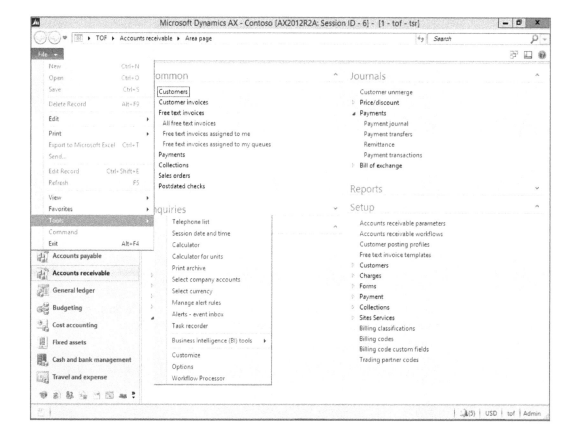

Log into Dynamics AX as an administrator, and from the **Files** menu of the Dynamics AX client, select the **Task Recorder** from the **Tools** submenu.

Accessing The Task Recorder

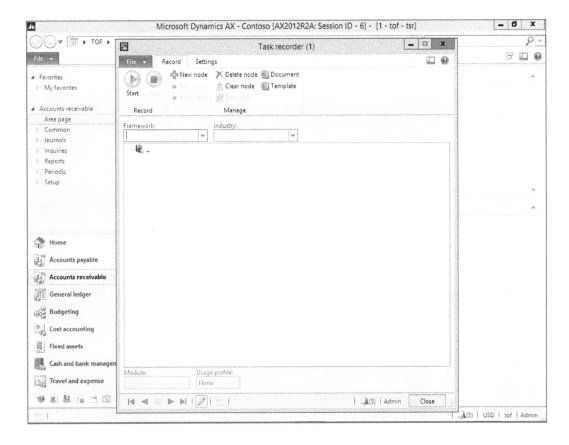

This will open up the new **Task Recorder** for you to use.

Configuring a New Task Recorder Framework

In order to create a new business process template we need to create a **Framework**. This will be the parent that we will use to for all of our workflow groups and activities.

Configuring a New Task Recorder Framework

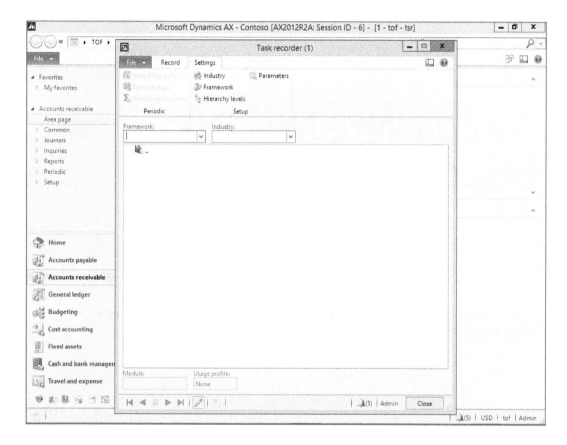

To do this, click on the **Framework** menu button from the **Setup** group of the **Setup** ribbon bar of the task recorder.

Configuring a New Task Recorder Framework

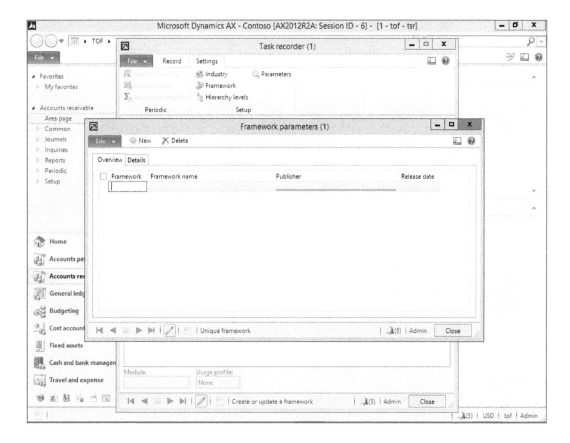

When the **Framework Parameters** maintenance form is displayed, click on the **New** button in the menu bar to create a new Framework record.

Configuring a New Task Recorder Framework

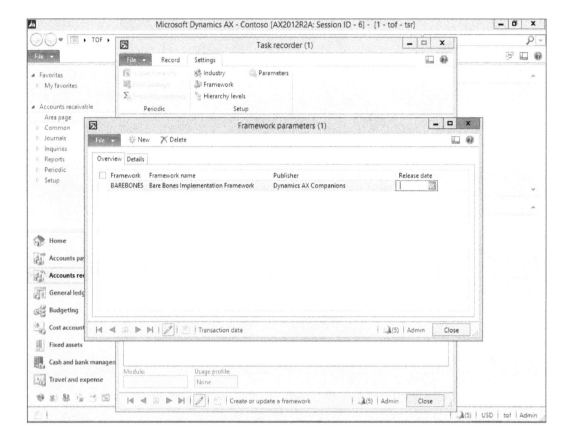

Assign your record a **Framework**, a **Framework name**, and a **Publisher**. When you have done that, click the **Close** button to exit the form.

Configuring a New Task Recorder Framework

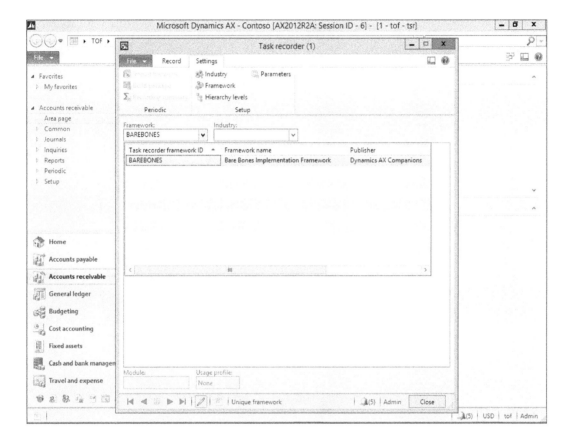

Now when you return to the Task Recorder, now you will see the new **Framework** record within the Framework drop down list.

Configuring a New Task Recorder Framework

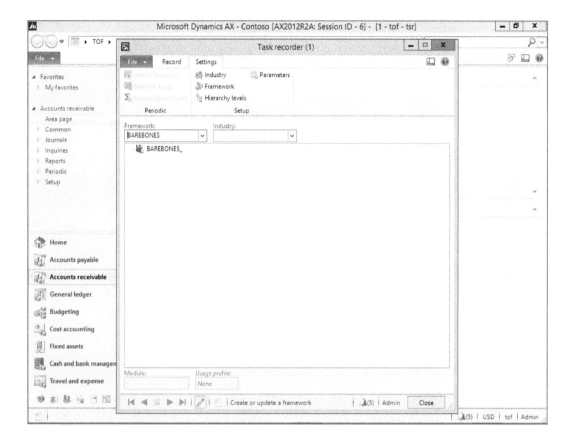

When you select the new Framework that you created, you will see an empty framework structure.

Defining Industry Codes

The Business Processes that you track within each **Framework** can also be split into different **Industry Codes** which us useful if you are working with different types of projects because the way that you perform tasks in one Industry may not be the same as in another.

So the next step that we need to perform is to configure an **Industry Code** for our task recording **Framework**.

Defining Industry Codes

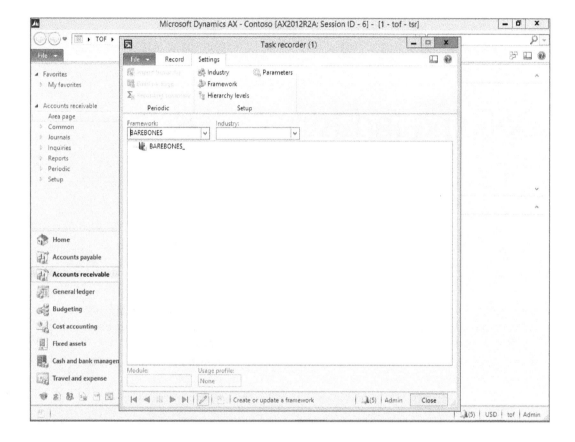

To do this, click on the **Industry** menu button from the **Setup** group of the **Setup** ribbon bar of the task recorder.

Defining Industry Codes

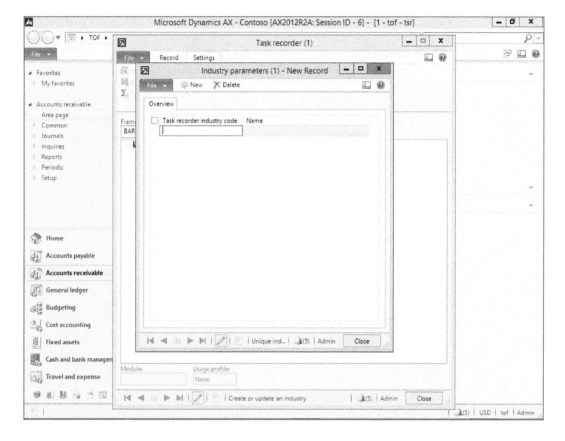

When the **Industry Parameters** dialog box is displayed, click on the **New** button in the menu bar to create a new Industry record.

Defining Industry Codes

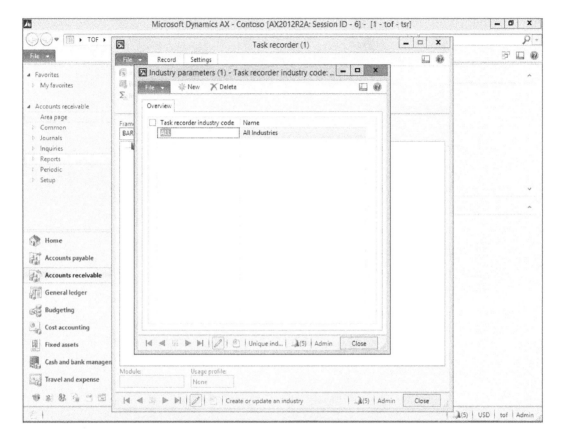

Give your new record a **Task Recorder Industry Code** and a **Name** and then click on the **Close** button to exit from the form.

Defining Industry Codes

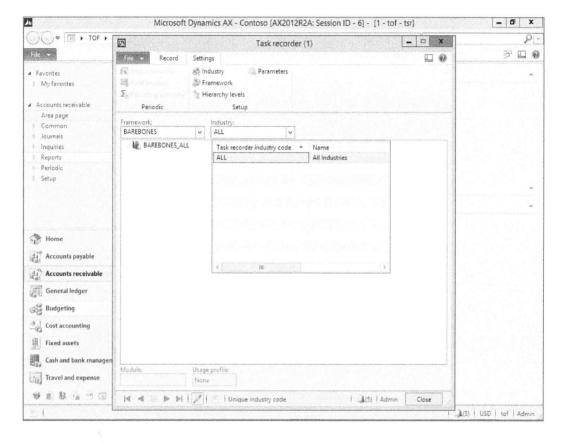

Now when you return to the Task Recorder, now you will see the new **Industry** record within the Framework drop down list.

Defining Industry Codes

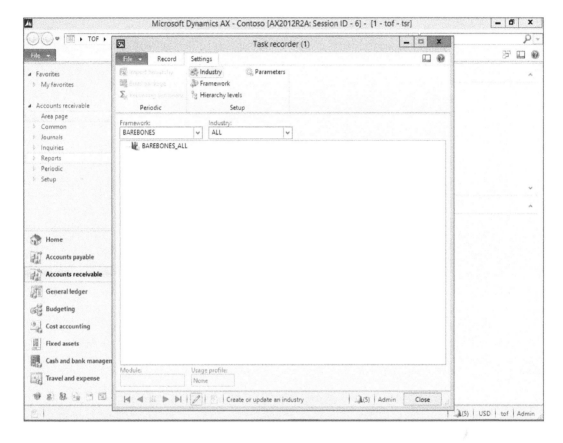

When you select the new **Industry** that you created, you will see an Industry is added to the parent tree structure.

Defining Hierarchy Levels for Your Framework

Before we start defining the groups and elements for our business process frameworks, we need to define the different process level. To do this we will create Hierarchy Levels within the task recorder.

In this example we will show how to define your business process hierarchies.

Defining Hierarchy Levels for Your Framework

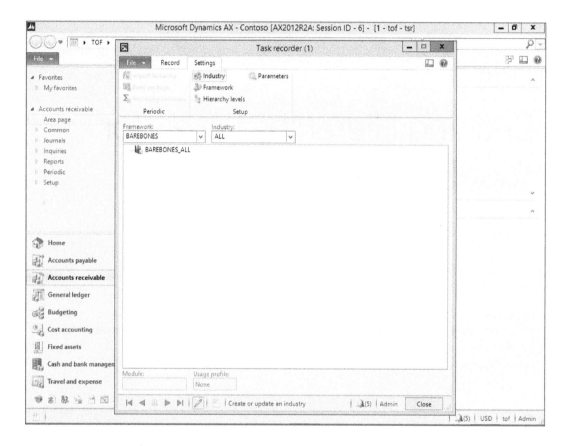

Open up the Task Recorder, and click on the **Hierarchy levels** menu within the **Setup** group of the **Setup** ribbon bar.

Defining Hierarchy Levels for Your Framework

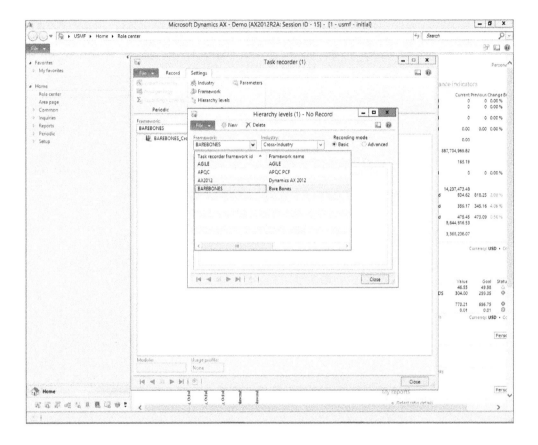

When the **Hierarchy levels** dialog box is displayed, select the **Framework** and **Industry** that you want to update from the dropdown list.

Defining Hierarchy Levels for Your Framework

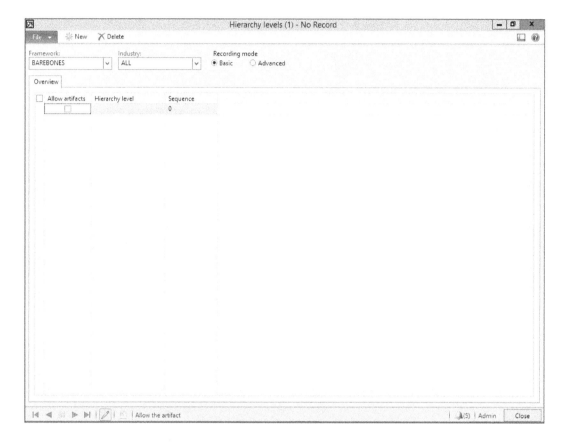

To create a new **Hierarchy level** click on the **New** item within the menu bar.

Defining Hierarchy Levels for Your Framework

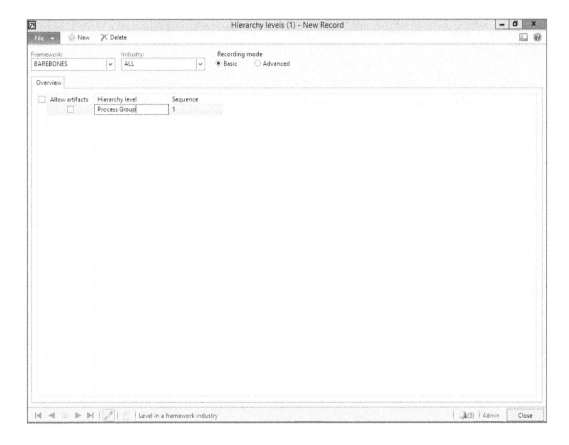

Set the name within the **Hierarchy level** field, and also the **Sequence** level.

Defining Hierarchy Levels for Your Framework

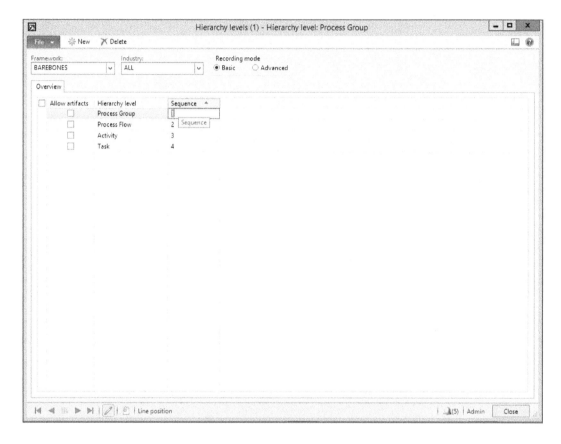

Repeat the process to add in all of the levels that you will be using in your business processes.

Defining Hierarchy Levels for Your Framework

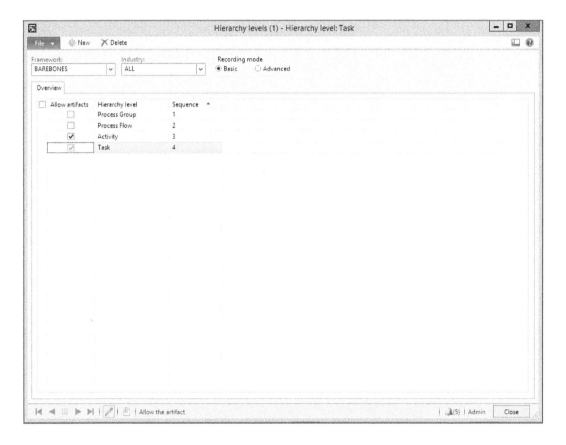

If you want to be able to attach documents (a.k.a. artifacts) against your business process levels, then mark the levels by checking the **Allow artifacts** check boxes.

Defining Hierarchy Levels for Your Framework

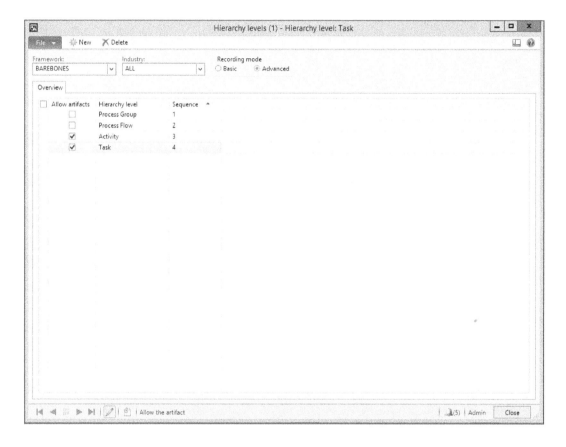

Finally, after you have defined the Hierarchy levels, change the **Recording Mode** radio button option to **Advanced**. This will enable the exporting options that we will be using later on in this process.

When you have finished, just click the **Close** button to exit out of the form.

Building Your Business Process Framework Structure

Once you have your Framework, and Hierarchy levels defined, you can now start building your business process levels by creating **Framework nodes**. These will allow you to create the structure that will be copied over to the business processes within the Lifecycle Services.

In this example we will show you how to create a new business process structure by creating **Framework Nodes**.

Building Your Business Process Framework Structure

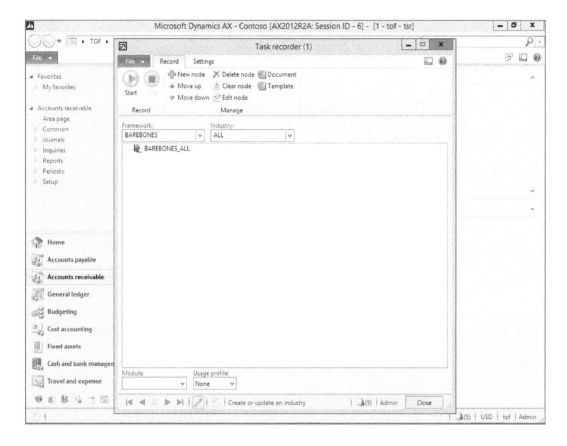

Open up the **Task Recorder**, and select the **Framework** that you want to update and click on **New** node menu item from within the **Manage** group of the **Record** ribbon bar of the Task Recorder.

Building Your Business Process Framework Structure

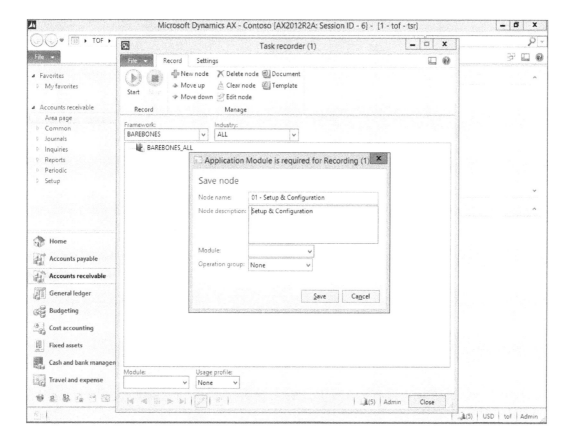

When the **Save node** dialog box is displayed, set the **Node name**. You can also add a **Node description**, a **Module** and also an **Operation group**. Then click the **Save** button to add the node to the framework.

Building Your Business Process Framework Structure

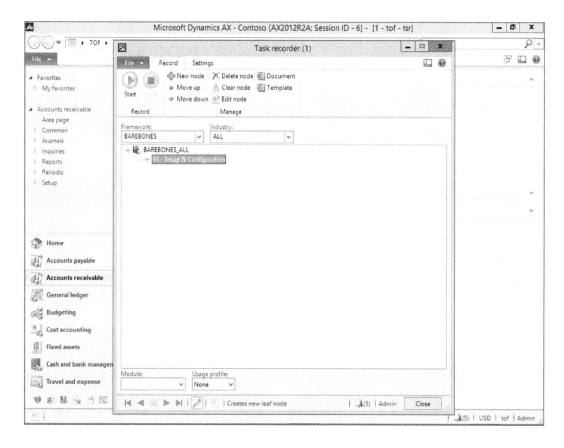

This will add a node under the parent node within the Task Recorder hierarchy.

Building Your Business Process Framework Structure

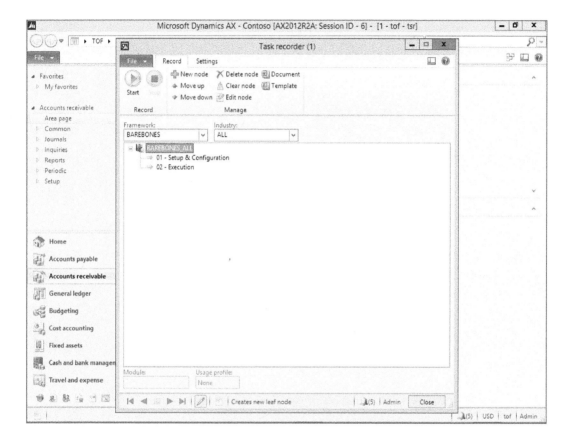

Repeat the process for any other base processes that you want to add to your business process.

Building Your Business Process Framework Structure

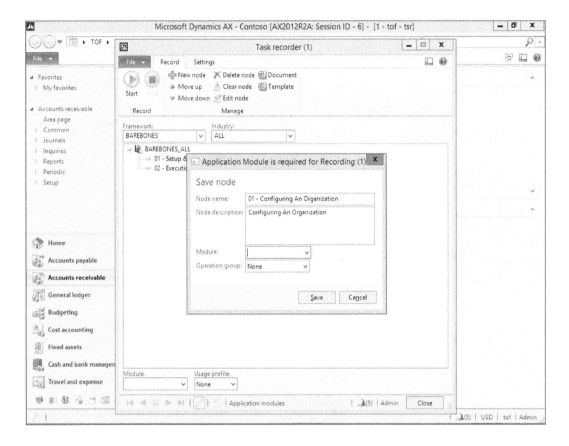

To add sub-nodes to your business processes, just select an existing node, and click on the **New node** menu item from within the **Manage** group of the **Record** ribbon bar of the Task Recorder.

When the **Save node** dialog box is displayed, set the **Node name**. You can also add a **Node description**.

Building Your Business Process Framework Structure

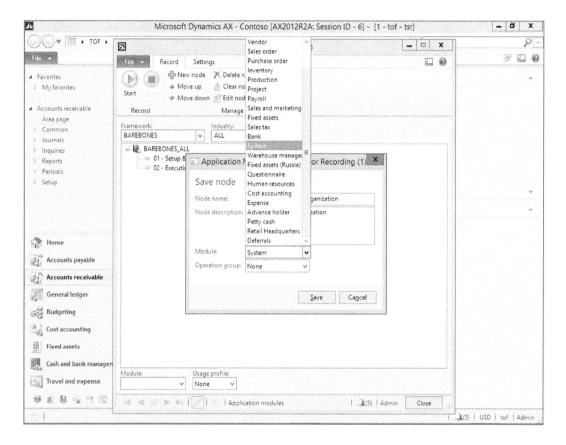

Select a **Module**

Building Your Business Process Framework Structure

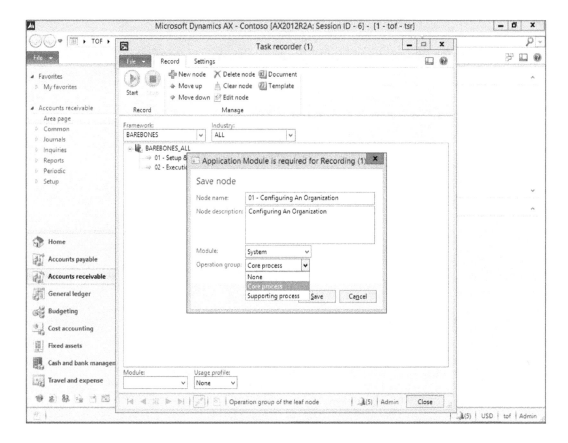

And also an **Operation group**.

Building Your Business Process Framework Structure

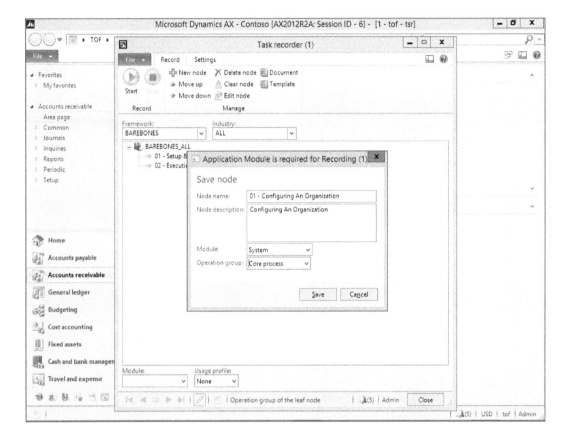

Then click the **Save** button to add the node to the framework.

Building Your Business Process Framework Structure

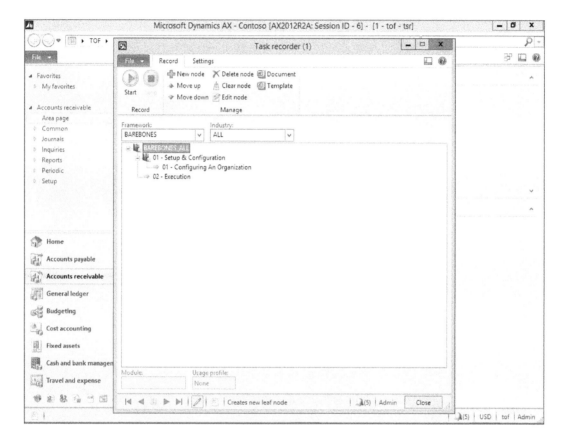

Now you will have a second level node within your hierarchy.

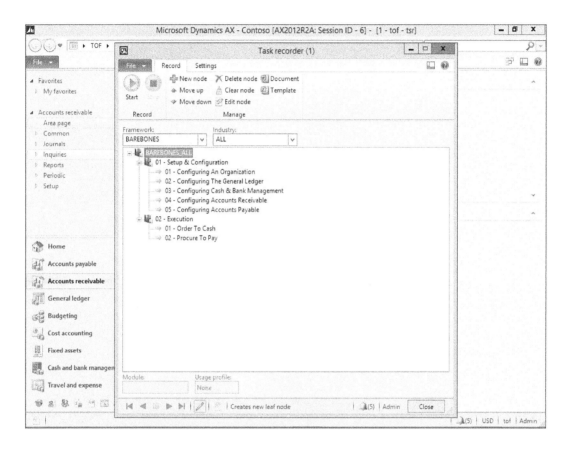

You can keep on adding nodes at this level as well.

Building Your Business Process Framework Structure

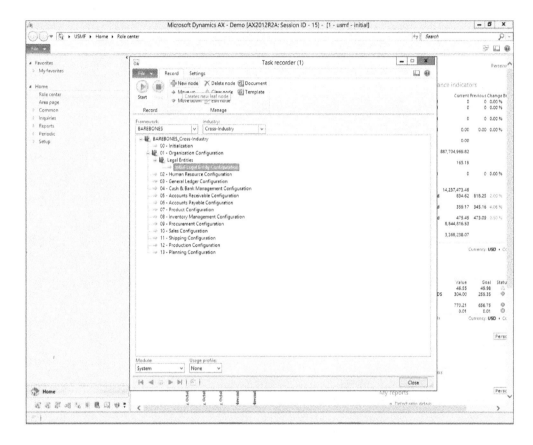

You can select the child node that you created, you can create additional sub levels exactly the same way.

Building Your Business Process Framework Structure

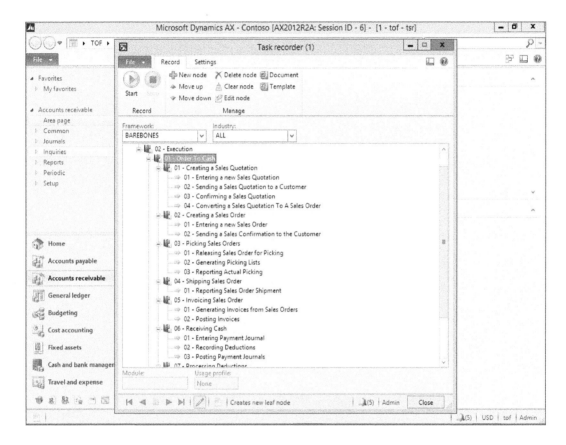

You can repeat the node creation steps to fill out all of the business process stages for your framework.

Creating a Business Process Import Template

If you have a pre-defined business process that you want to set up within the Task Recorder Framework, but you don't want to type them in by hand, then you can create a template file within Excel and then use the import function within the Task Recorder to save time.

In this example we will show you how to create a template that you can then use as an import template for the Task Recorder frameworks.

Creating a Business Process Import Template

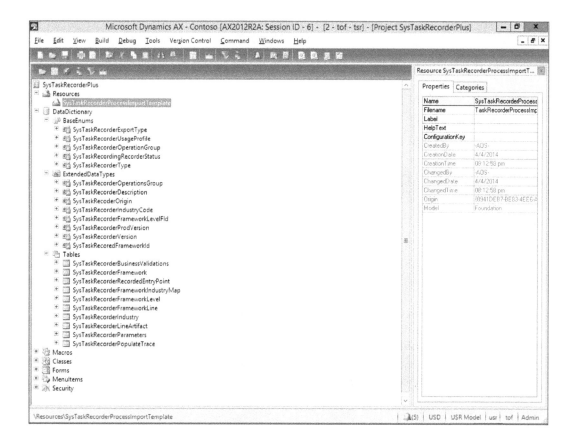

To create the initial Excel workbook with all of the right columns and formatting, there is a utility hidden away within AOT called **Task Recorder Plus**. To access it, open up AOT and then the project browser (CTRL+SHIFT+P), and find the public project called **SysTaskRecorderPlus**.

Then right-mouse-click on the **SysTaskRecorderProcessImportTemplate** resource, and select the **Open** option.

Creating a Business Process Import Template

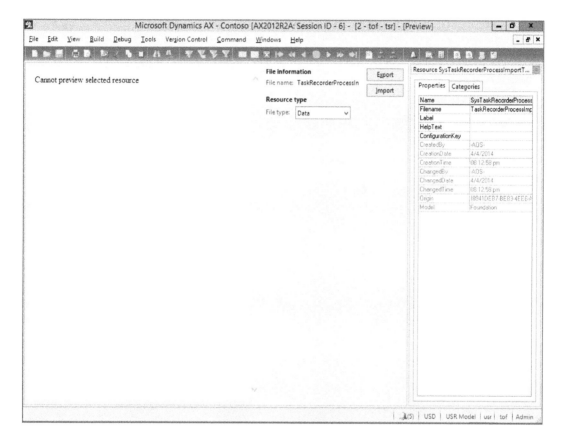

When the Process Import Template dialog box is displayed, click on the **Export** button.

Creating a Business Process Import Template

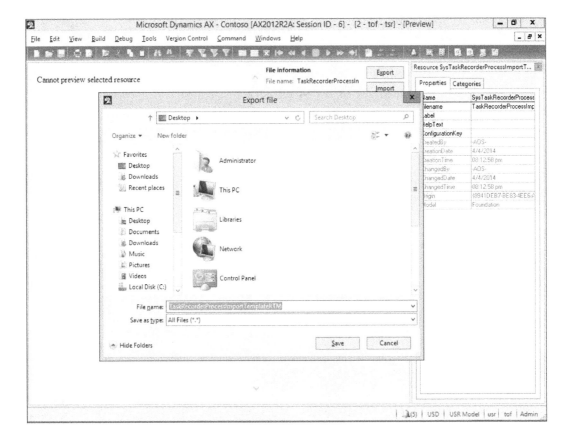

When the file explorer is displayed, set the location that you want to store the template, and then click the **Save** button.

Creating a Business Process Import Template

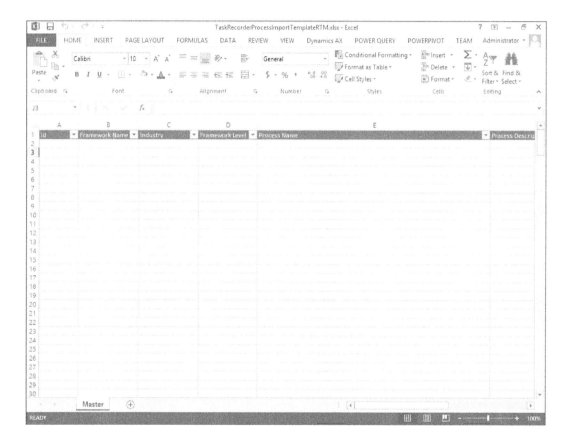

Now you can open up the template file that it created for you and you will be able to see that all of the required columns are set up in the worksheet.

Creating a Business Process Import Template

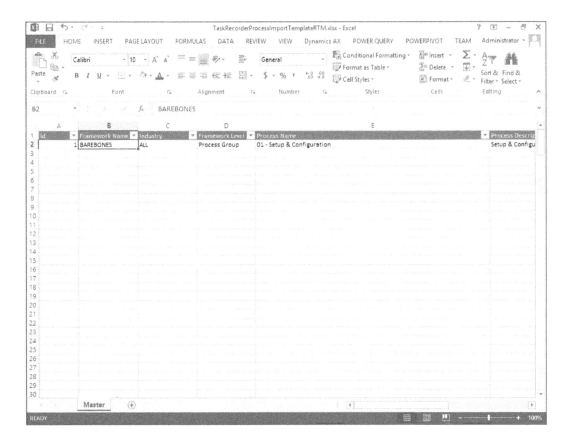

All you need to do is start entering in each of the Business Process levels the spreadsheet.

Creating a Business Process Import Template

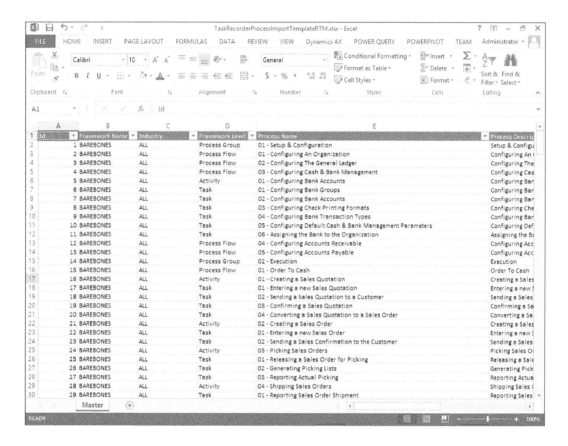

Keep on adding in all of the nodes.

Note: You may need to tweak the data a little. The tweaks that you will probably have to do by hand will be setting the **Process Level** to match the **Hierarchy Levels** that you defined in the previous steps. Also, you will need to define the **Parent Id** the node to link back to.

After you have created the template, you can save and close the file.

Importing a Business Process Framework from a Template

Once you have a template file defined, you can then import directly into the Task Recorder hierarchy, saving you a lot of manual work in typing in the individual nodes.

In this example we will show how to import in a hierarchy template into the Task Recorder.

Importing a Business Process Framework from a Template

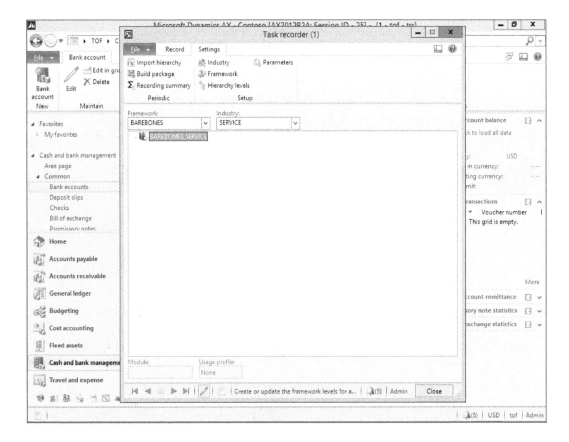

Open up the Task Recorder, select the blank Framework that you want to import the template into.

Click on the **Import hierarchy** menu item within the **Periodic** group of the **Settings** ribbon bar.

Note: If these items are disabled, then it is probably because when you defined the **Hierarchy Levels** you did not check the **Advanced** option.

Importing a Business Process Framework from a Template

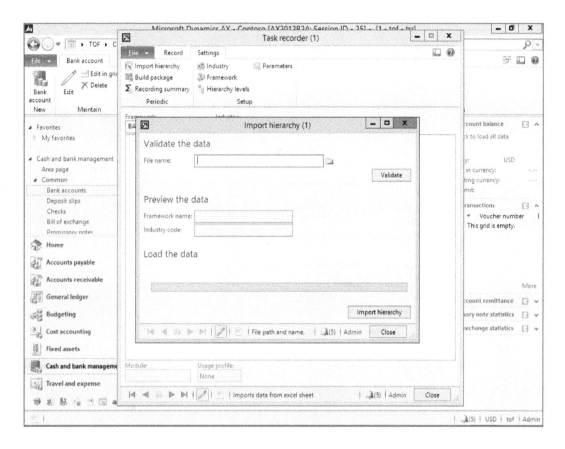

This will open up the **Import Hierarchy** dialog box. Click on the folder icon to the right of the **Filename** field so that we can point it to our new template.

Importing a Business Process Framework from a Template

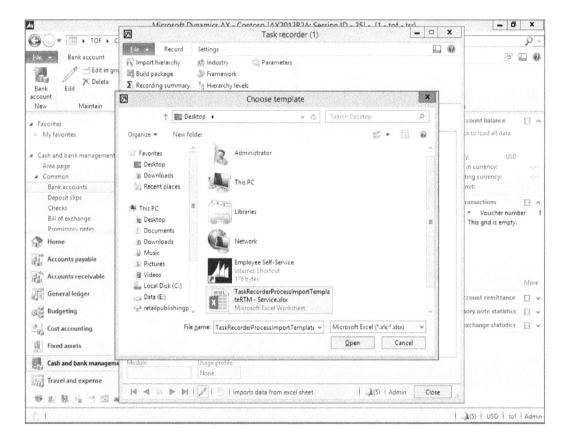

When the file explorer dialog box is displayed, find the Excel template file that you just created and then click the **Open** button.

Importing a Business Process Framework from a Template

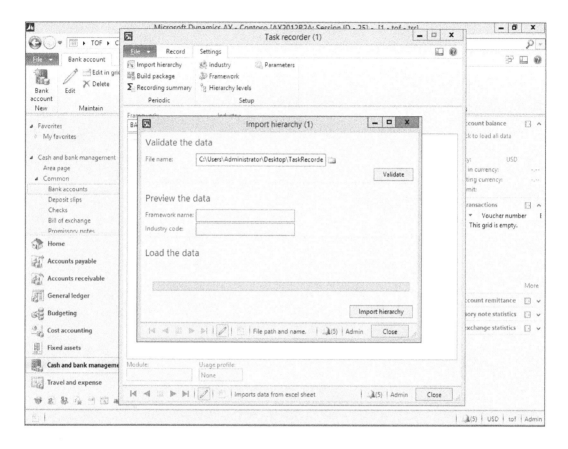

Now click on the **Validate** button so that the Task Recorder is able to review the file for you.

Importing a Business Process Framework from a Template

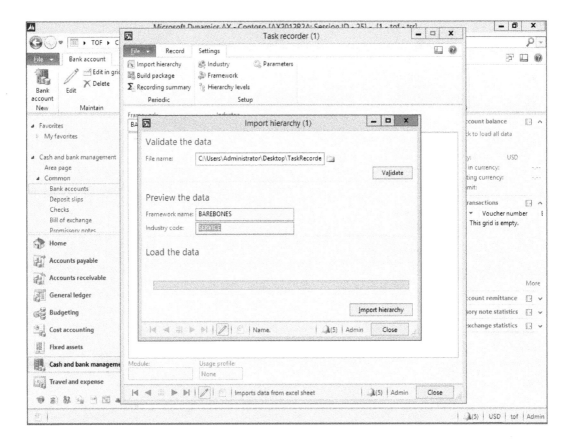

If everything is OK, then it will populate the **Framework name**, and **Industry code**.

When the file is successfully validated, click on the **Import hierarchy** button to start the import process.

Importing a Business Process Framework from a Template

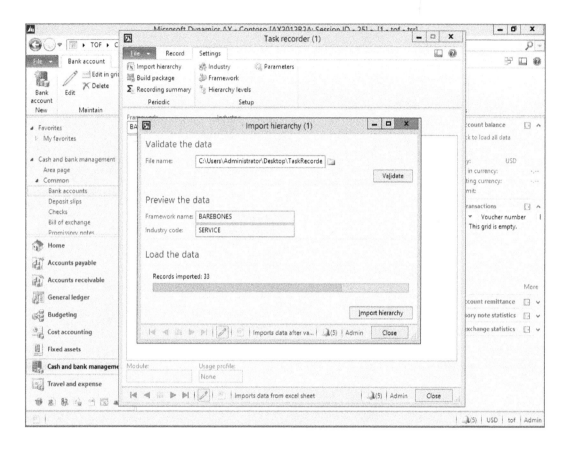

The import will run for a little bit and load in all of the records from the template.

Importing a Business Process Framework from a Template

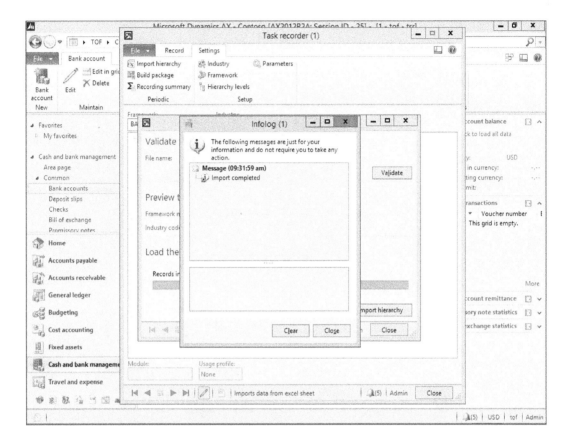

If everything is OK then you will get a InfoLog from the system.

Importing a Business Process Framework from a Template

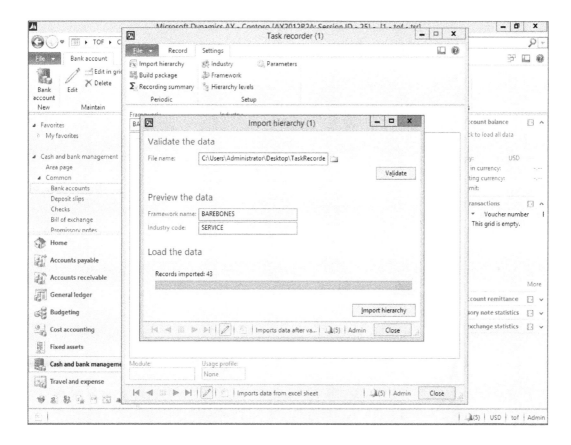

Then you can ou can click the **Close** button to exit out of the form.

Importing a Business Process Framework from a Template

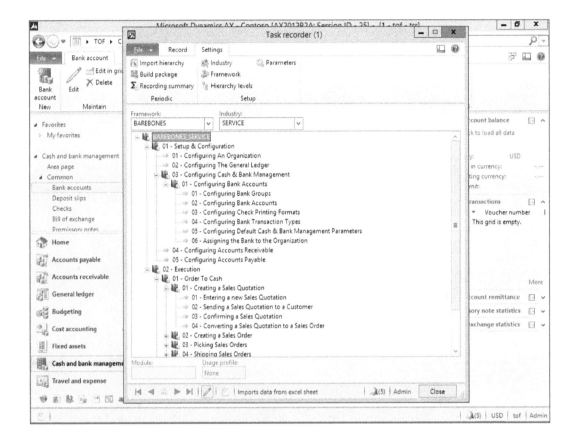

Then you return to the Task Recorder and refresh the framework, you should see that all of the nodes have been created for you.

Tip: You may need to check the sub-nodes of the Framework to make sure that all of the Parent Id relationships are correctly linked up. If you find a mistake, then you can just delete and recreate the Framework, update the template, and then re-import.

Configuring The Task Recorder Recording Parameters

There is one final step left before we can start using the task recorder and that is just to set some of the default parameters.

Configuring The Task Recorder Recording Parameters

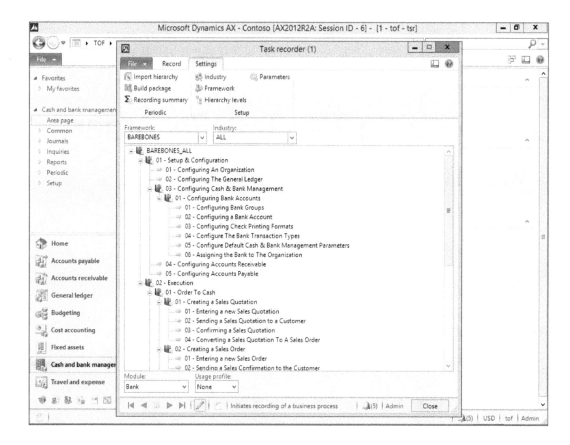

To do this, just click on the **Parameters** menu item within the **Setup** group of the **Settings** ribbon bar.

Configuring The Task Recorder Recording Parameters

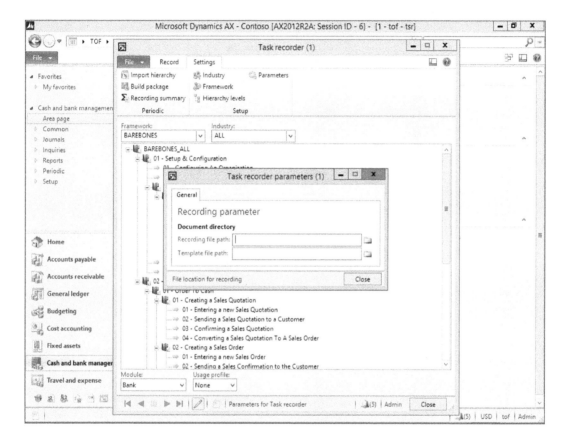

When the **Task Recorder Parameters** dialog box is displayed, click on the folder icon to the right of the **Recording File Path** field.

Configuring The Task Recorder Recording Parameters

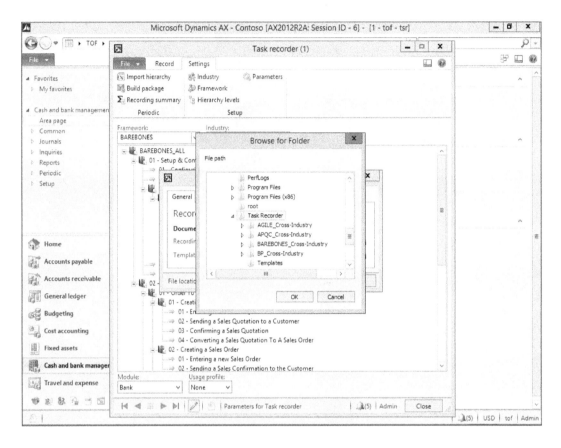

When the folder explorer is displayed, navigate to a shared location where you want to store all of the Task Recording detail and then click the **OK** button.

Configuring The Task Recorder Recording Parameters

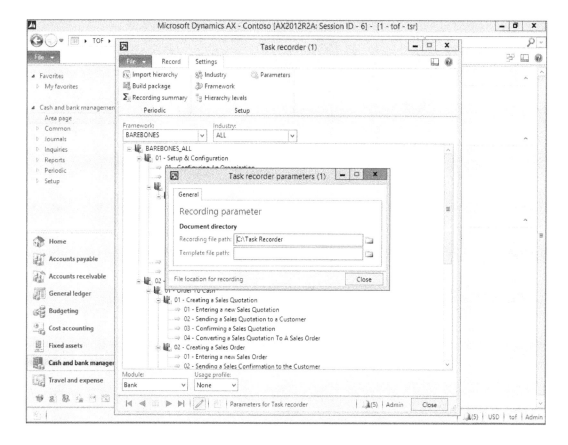

Then click on the folder icon to the right of the **Template File Path** field.

Configuring The Task Recorder Recording Parameters

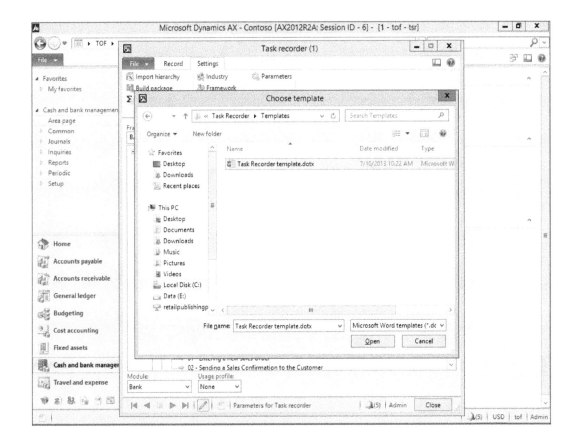

Browse to the location where you are storing your template file for your recordings, select the template and then click on the **Open** button.

Configuring The Task Recorder Recording Parameters

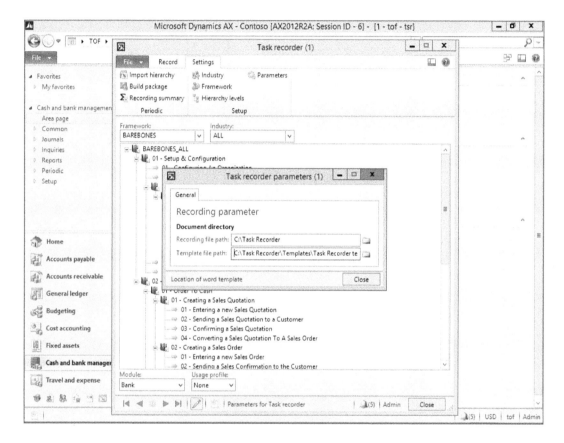

Now you are done, just click on the **Close** button to save the updates.

Recording A Task For a Business Process Element

The most valuable function that is built into the Task Recorder is that can use it to record the steps that you perform within Dynamics AX, and then store them against the task nodes within the Framework. These recordings are available and can be exported out as word documents, but also are exported to the Lifecycle Services portal and converted into business process diagrams for future reference. But in order to take advantage of this you need to record the task first.

In this example we will show you how to record a task within the Task Recorder.

Recording A Task For a Business Process Element

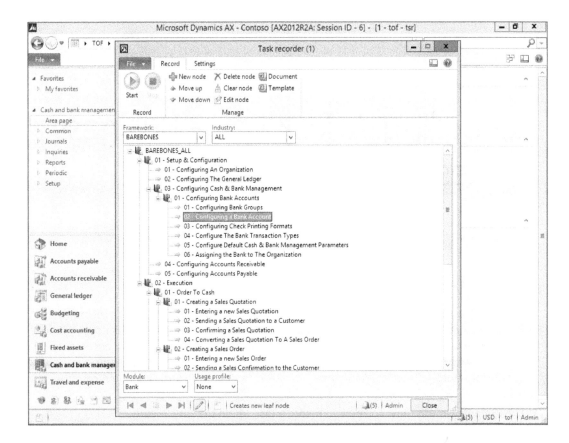

Select the node in the framework that you want to record your task against, and click on the
Start button within the **Record** group of the **Record** ribbon bar.

Recording A Task For a Business Process Element

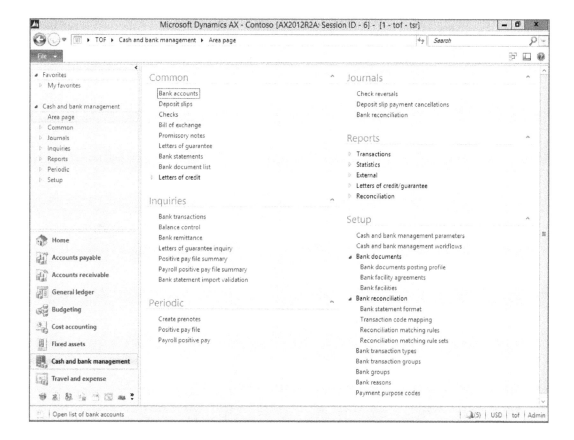

This will hide the Task Recorder and take you to the Dynamics AX client.

Note: You need to start on an Area Page for all recordings. If you don't then you will get a cryptic message saying that it will not record the images and your task recording won't look very good.

Recording A Task For a Business Process Element

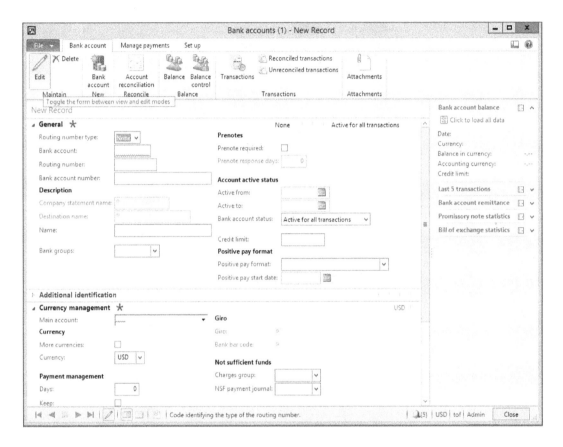

Now just run through your process that you want to record.

Recording A Task For a Business Process Element

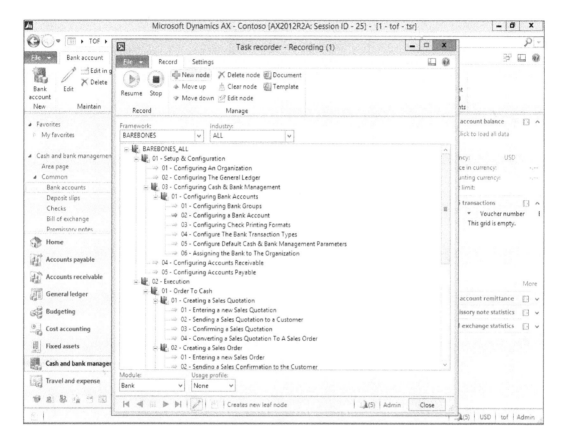

When you have finished the task, return to the **Task Recorder** and click on the **Stop** button within the **Record** group within the **Record** ribbon bar.

The task recorder will process for a little bit and then the arrow to the right of the task name will become full color indicating that the recording has been processed.

Printing Out The Task Recording Documentation

Once you have created the **Task Recording** then you can get the system to create your documentation for you by exporting it to Word.

Printing Out The Task Recording Documentation

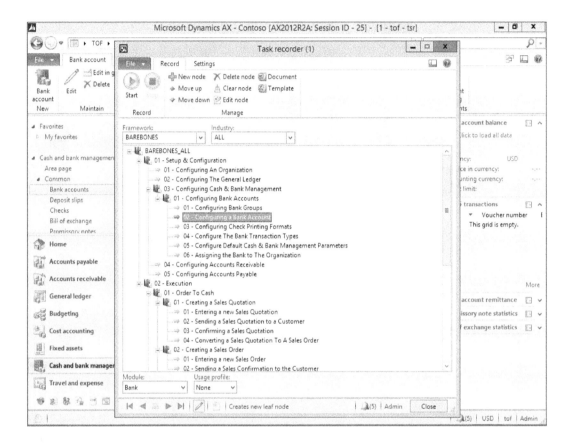

To do this, just select the task that you want to create the document from and click on the **Document** menu item within the **Manage** group of the **Record** ribbon bar.

Printing Out The Task Recording Documentation

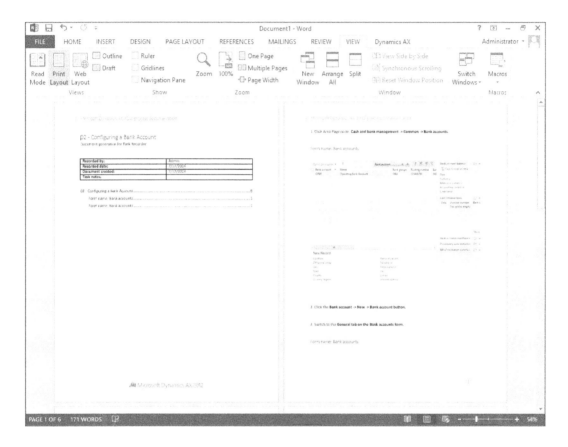

The Task Recorder will automatically open up Word using the template that you linked to within the Task Recorder Parameters and build the documentation for you creating a cover page and also embedding in all of the images from the recording.

Very cool!

Customizing The Task Recorder Word Template

If you want to spiff up the documentation a little then you can reformat the template that is used by the Task Recorder and add your own flair to it.

Customizing The Task Recorder Word Template

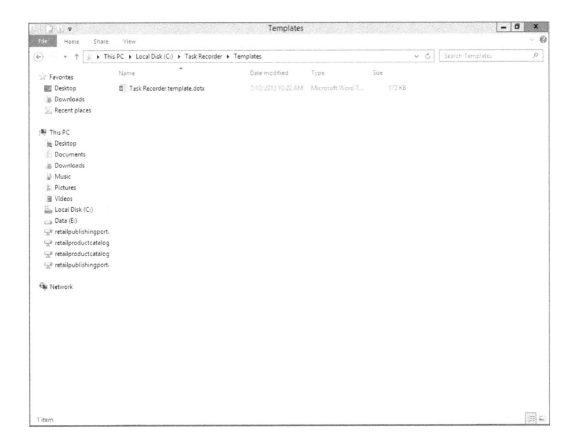

To do this, find the location where the default Task Recorder Word Template is stored and open up the template file.

Customizing The Task Recorder Word Template

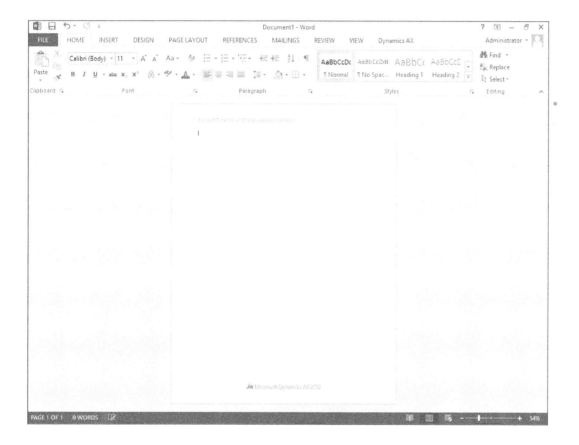

When the template opens up you will notice that it already had the header and footer details for the document – although it looks a little boring.

Customizing The Task Recorder Word Template

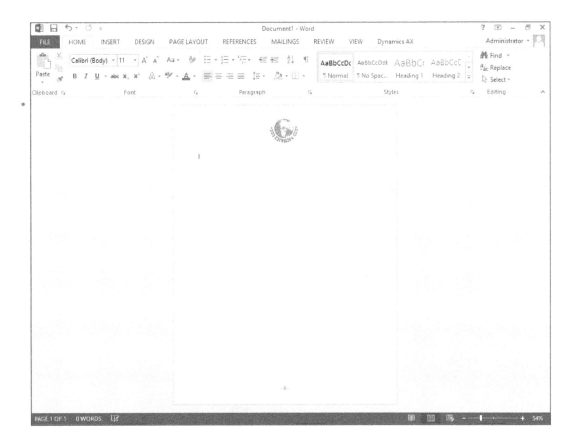

Just update the template and add in your own header and footer, and any other default information that you want to show on the outputted documents.

Customizing The Task Recorder Word Template

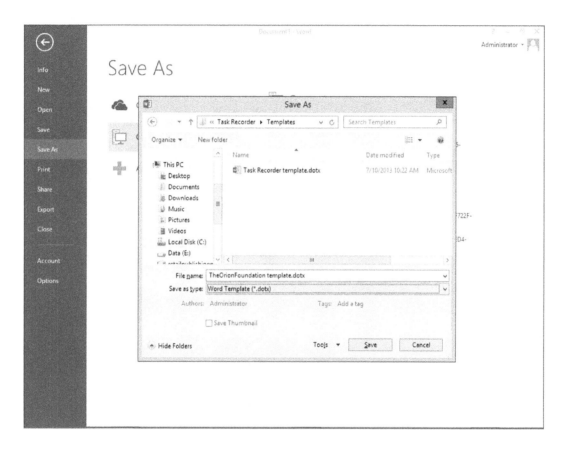

Then resave the file as a **.dotx** document template.

Customizing The Task Recorder Word Template

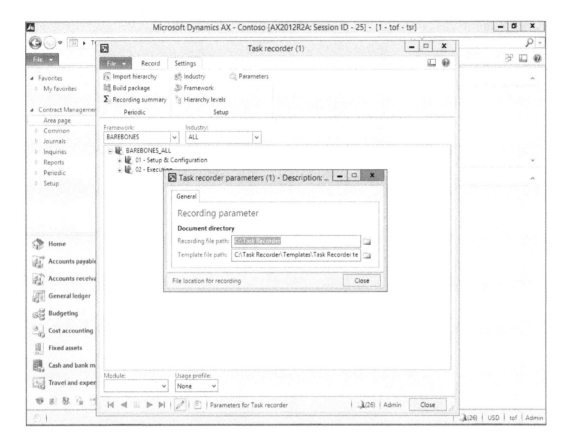

If you have changed the name of the template, then you will also want to go back to the **Task Recorder Parameters** and update the **Template File Path.**

Customizing The Task Recorder Word Template

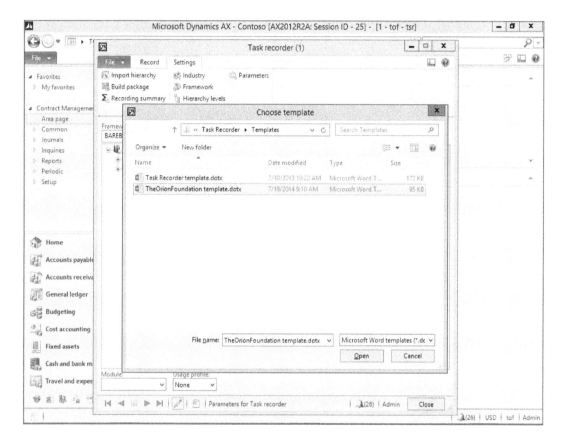

Just point it to your new template file and click the **Open** button.

Customizing The Task Recorder Word Template

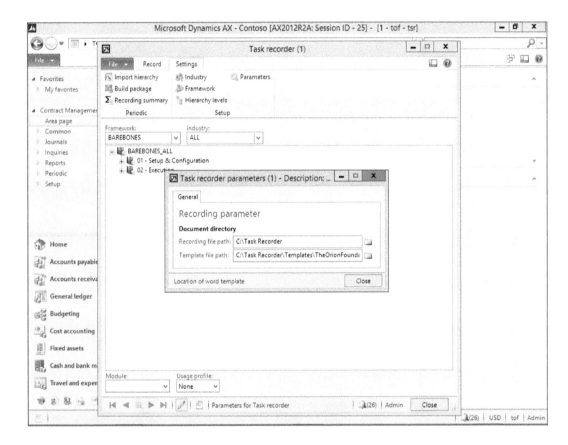

After you have done that, click the **Close** button to exit from the form.

Customizing The Task Recorder Word Template

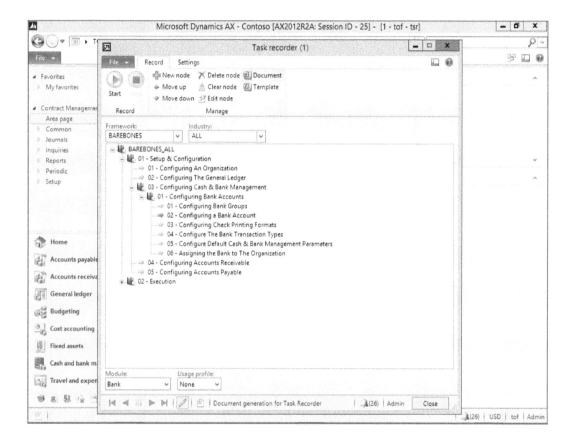

Now select the node that you want to create the documentation for and click on the **Document** button within the **Manage** group of the **Record** ribbon bar.

Customizing The Task Recorder Word Template

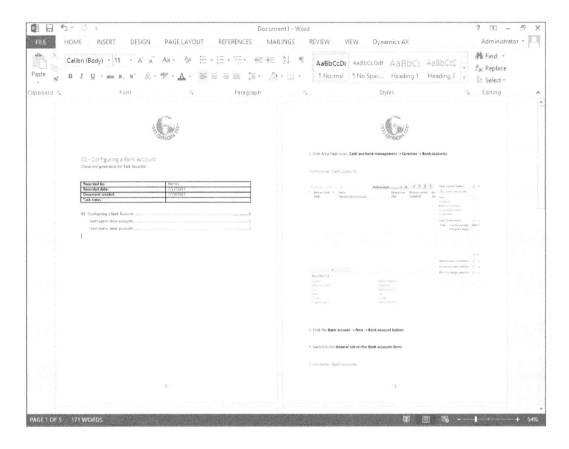

Now your documentation will have your own template look and feel.

That looks much better ☺

Creating A Data Entry Template From A Task Recording

One other documentation tool that you can use within the **Task Recorder** is the function that will create your own data entry templates. Because the **Task Recorder** knows what fields you have updated as you went through the recording process, it is able to create a blank Excel template file that you can then update off-line with your record values, and then others are able to use this as a reference for setting up the data.

Creating A Data Entry Template From A Task Recording

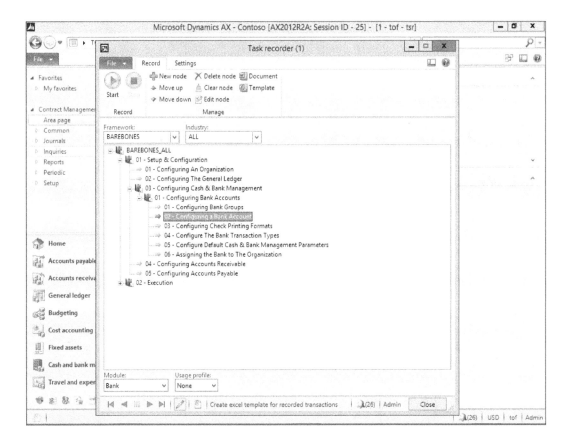

All you need to do is select the Task Recording node that you want to create the template for and click on the **Template** button within the **Manage** group of the **Record** ribbon bar.

Creating A Data Entry Template From A Task Recording

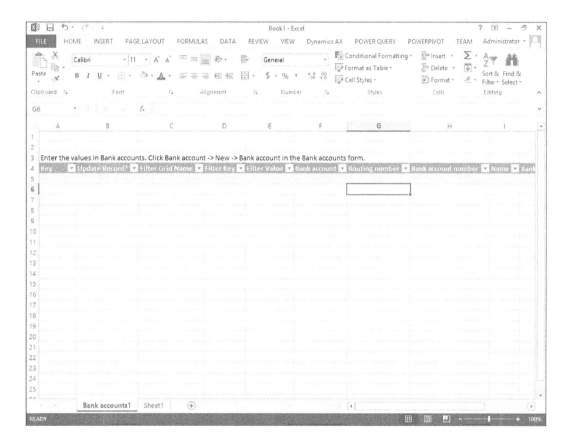

The Task Recorder will create an Excel Workbook for you with all of the key fields that you updated during the recording phase.

Creating A Data Entry Template From A Task Recording

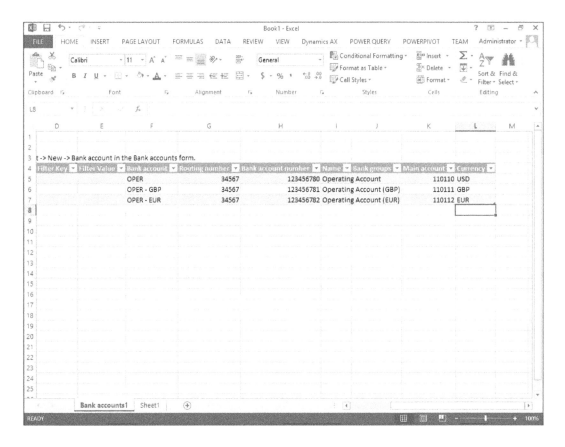

To create your template, just fill in the information in the key fields.

Creating A Data Entry Template From A Task Recording

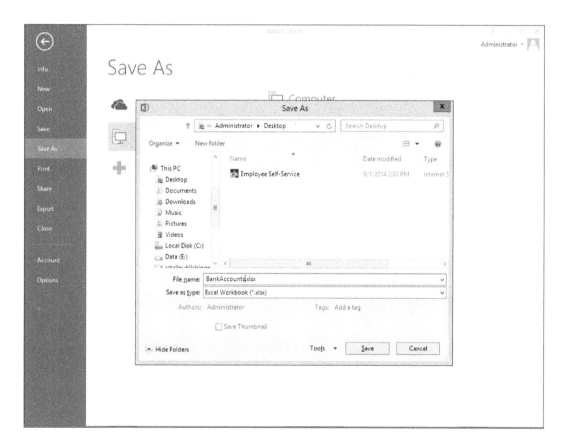

After you have done this, it might be a good idea to save the file away so that we can reference it later on.

Accessing Task Recording Video

One other artifact that is created by the Task Recorder as you are recording the tasks are videos that record everything that you are doing in real time. If you want to access these to use for other training material then go for it – all you need to know is where they are stored.

Accessing Task Recording Video

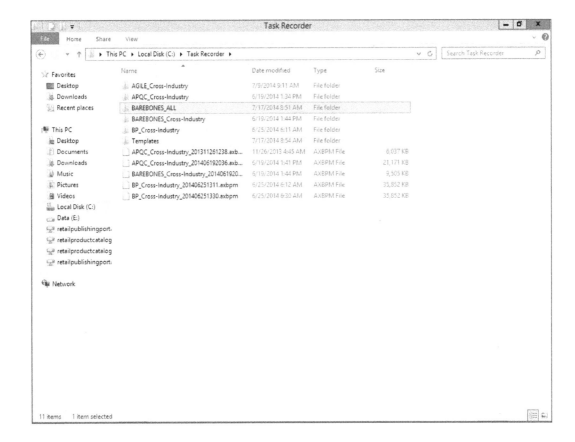

To find the videos, open up the folder that you identified to store all of the task recordings in when you configured the Parameters. You will notice that there are subfolders for all of the Framework & Industry combinations that you have created Task Recordings for.

Accessing Task Recording Video

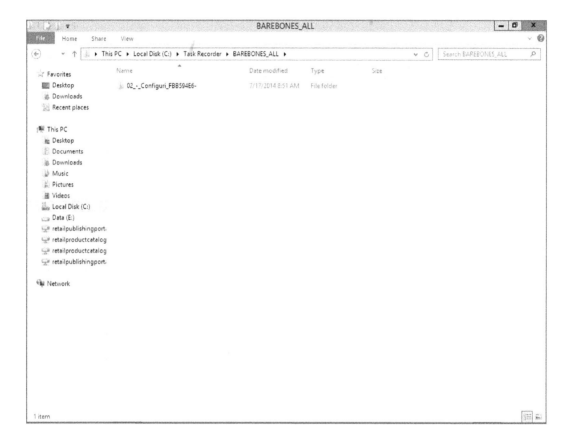

If you open up any of them you will find another folder for each of the Task Recordings that you have made.

Accessing Task Recording Video

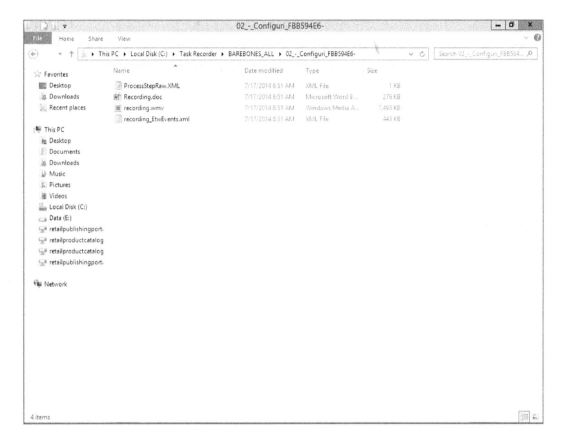

Drilling into those folders you will see that the Task Recorder automatically creates the Word documentation for you and also a recording.wmv file.

Accessing Task Recording Video

If you open up the recording.wmv file you will see that it is a verbatim recording of everything done during the task recording.

Time to post something on YouTube?

Building an Lifecycle Services import Package

Once you have created your framework within the Task Recorder, and recorded your business process tasks, you can get it ready to be used within the Lifecycle Services projects as a template business process model by creating an export file.

In this example we will show how you can create an export package for the Lifecycle Services business process.

Building an Lifecycle Services import Package

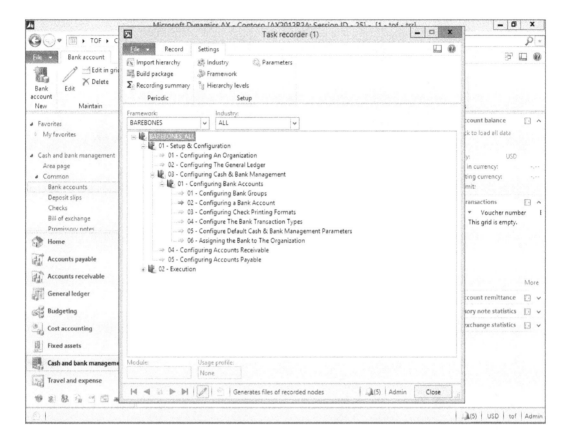

Open up the Task Recorder, and select the Framework that you want to create the export package for. Then click on the **Build package** menu item within the **Periodic** group of the **Settings** ribbon bar.

Building an Lifecycle Services import Package

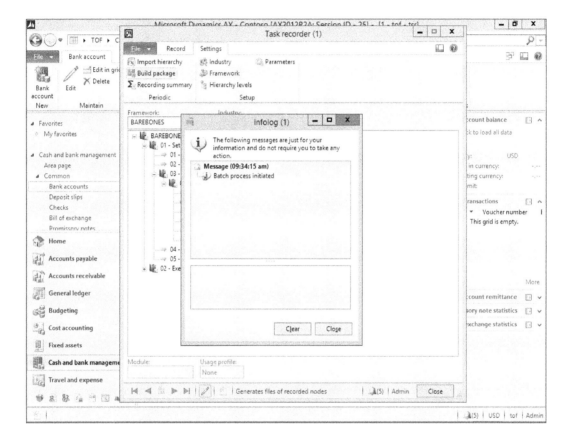

This will initiate a batch that will run in the background to create the package for you.

Building an Lifecycle Services import Package

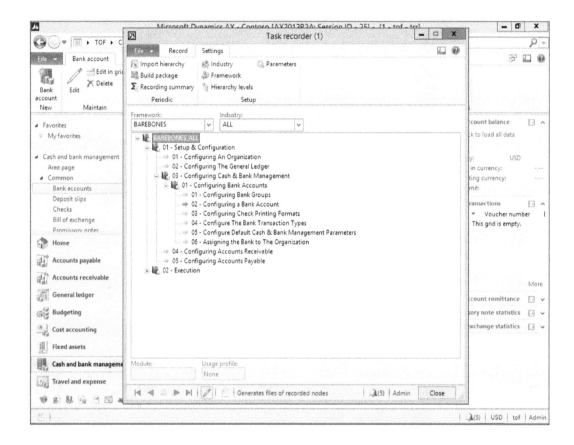

Tip: The export package will be stored within the default export directory of the Task Recorder. To find that location just click on the **Parameters** menu item within the **Setup** group of the **Settings** ribbon bar.

Building an Lifecycle Services import Package

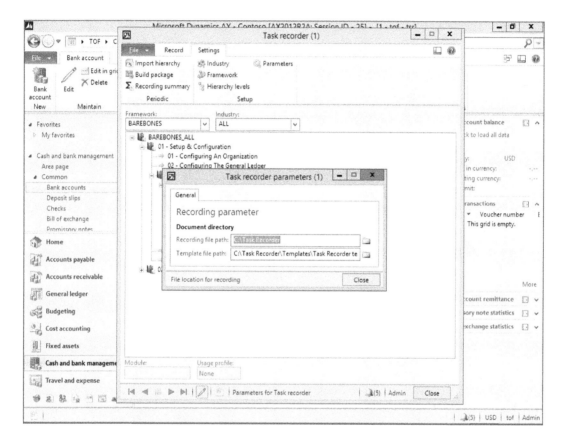

The file location will be shown in the **Recording file path** field.

Building an Lifecycle Services import Package

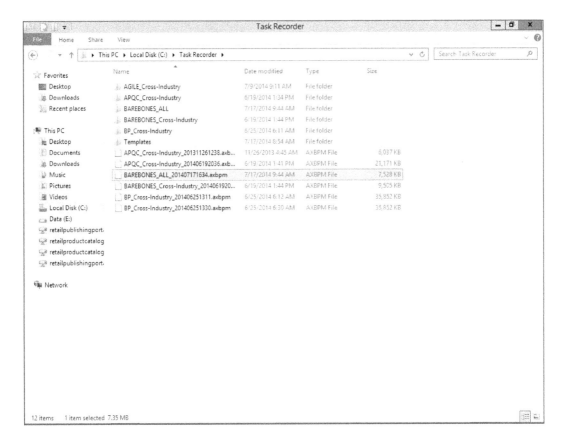

If you open up the Task Recorder folder, then you will be able to see all of the export packages that the Task Recorder created.

Importing the Business Process Package into a Lifecycle Services Project

Once you have a business process import package, you can import it into the Lifecycle Services so that you can use it as a template within your projects.

In this example we will show you how to import in a Task Recorder Framework package as Business Process.

Importing the Business Process Package into a Lifecycle Services Project

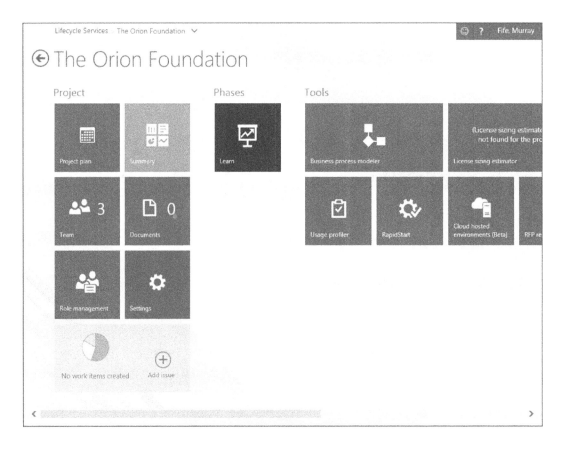

Log into Lifecycle Services, and click on the **Business process modeler** tile.

Importing the Business Process Package into a Lifecycle Services Project

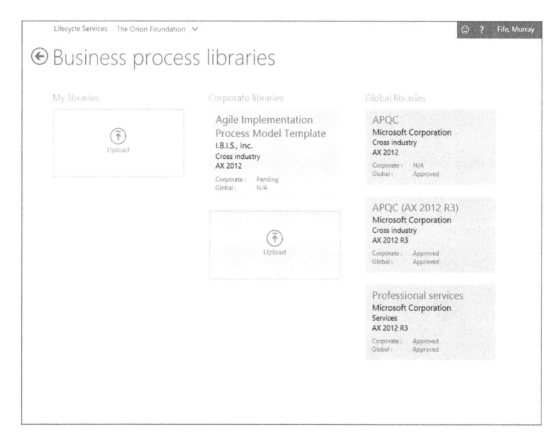

When the projects Business Process Library is displayed, click on the **Upload** link within the **My Projects** tile.

Importing the Business Process Package into a Lifecycle Services Project

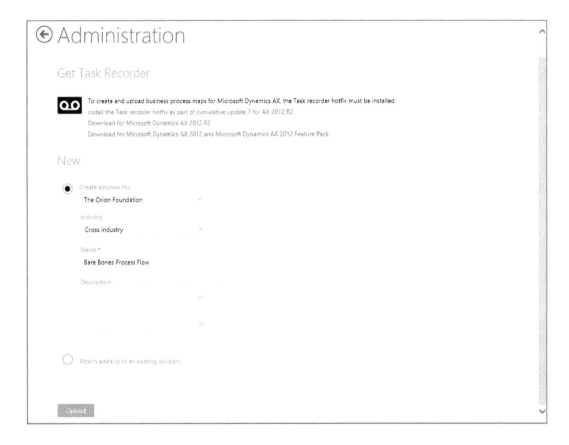

Give your business process template a **Name** and then click on the **Upload** button.

Importing the Business Process Package into a Lifecycle Services Project

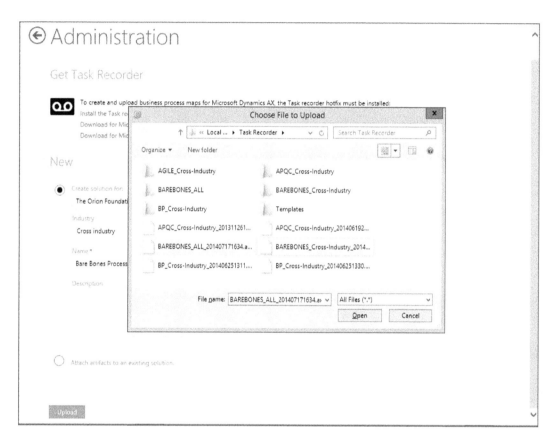

When the file explorer is displayed, navigate to the export package that the Task Recorder created and select it by clicking on the **Open** button.

Importing the Business Process Package into a Lifecycle Services Project

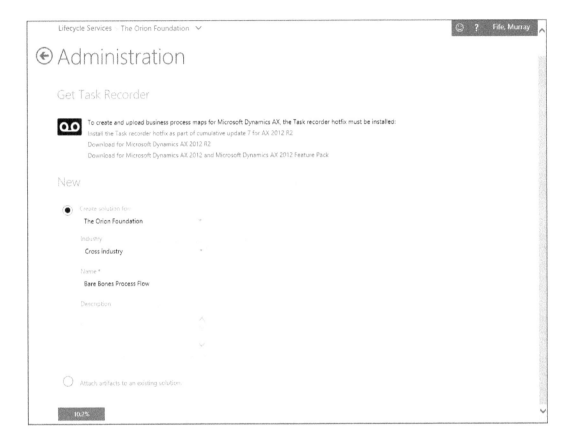

You should notice that it starts processing the Task Recording Package for you.

Importing the Business Process Package into a Lifecycle Services Project

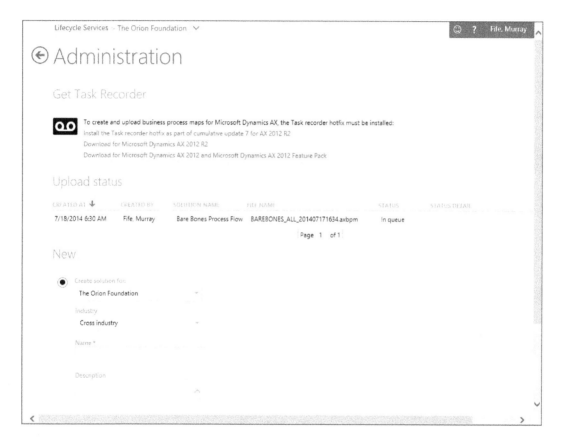

After a few minutes, the website will upload the package, and you will see that the package has a Status of **In queue**.

Importing the Business Process Package into a Lifecycle Services Project

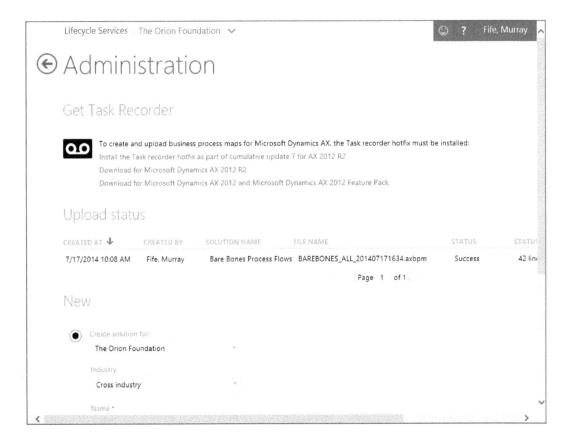

After a few minutes the Lifecycle Services will process the package, and the status will change to **Success**.

Importing the Business Process Package into a Lifecycle Services Project

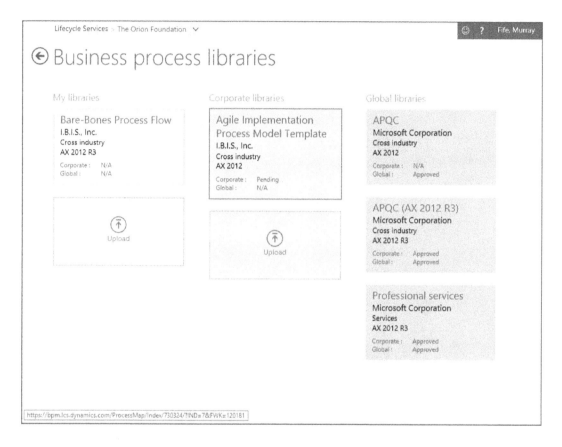

Now when you return back to the **Business process library** you will be able to see a new business process model has been added to the project.

Importing the Business Process Package into a Lifecycle Services Project

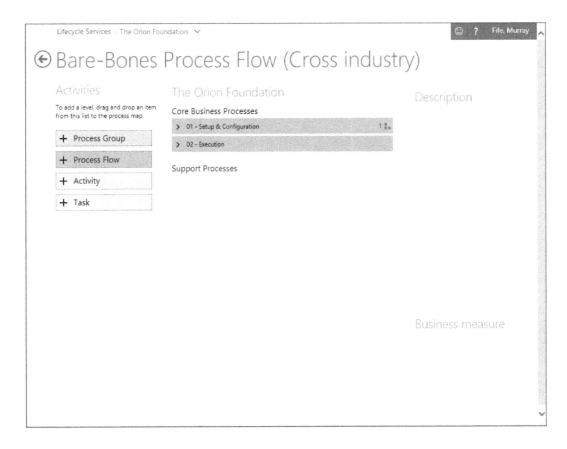

If you open up the business process then you will see the same structure that you have built within the Task Recorder.

Importing the Business Process Package into a Lifecycle Services Project

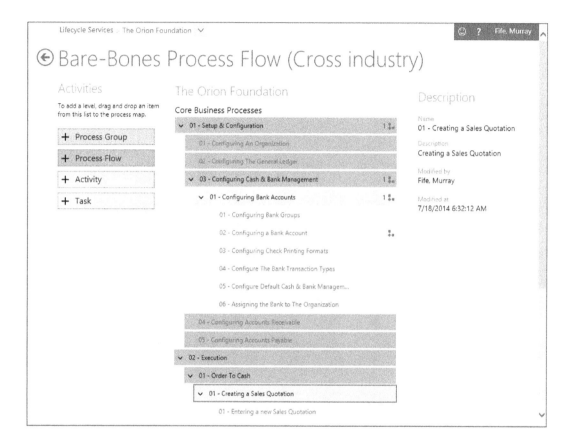

You can drill into the levels and see all of the sub items and activities.

Note: the level names will be the names that you configured within the **Hierarchy levels** within the task recorder.

Also if you have some task recordings, the you will see a small flowchart icon to the right of the business process level.

Importing the Business Process Package into a Lifecycle Services Project

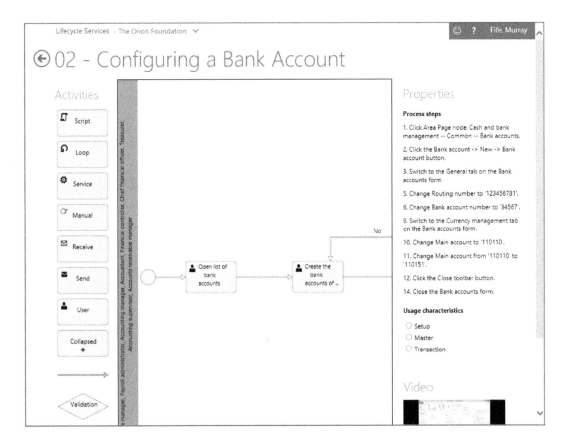

If you click on the flowchart icon within the process model, it will open up a visual diagram of the task that you recorded. On the right you will see the narrative of the process, and also a thumbnail of a video that was recorded of the task as it was recorded.

Importing the Business Process Package into a Lifecycle Services Project

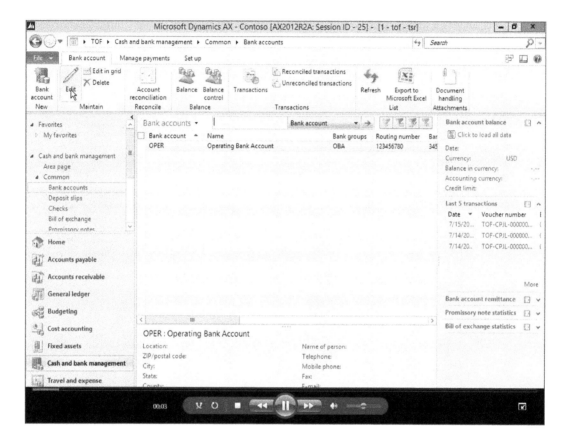

Expanding out the video will show you the business process in action.

Importing the Business Process Package into a Lifecycle Services Project

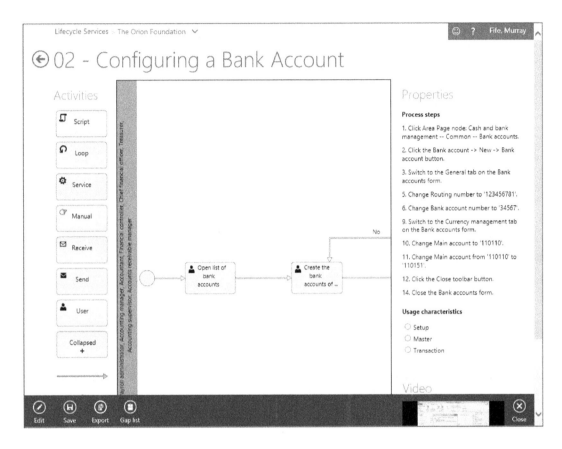

If you right-mouse-click on the workspace of the form, then a menu will beat the bottom of the page. If you click on the **Export** menu button it will export the business process Visio.

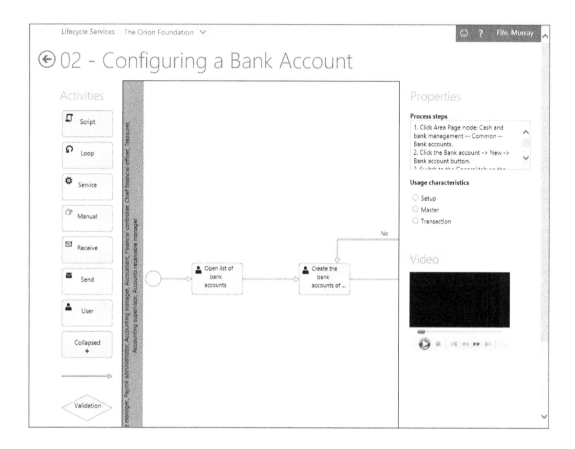

Importing Business Process Flows From Other Libraries

You have probably noticed that there are a number of standard Business Process Flows that are available within Lifecycle Services, and if you wanted to you could use them as your standard Business Process Flows within your custom business model by importing them into your model. This allows you to add best practice models without having to record them manually yourself.

Importing Business Process Flows From Other Libraries

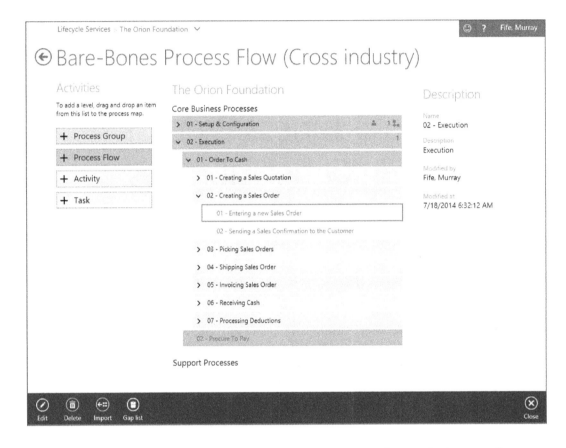

To do this, right-mouse-click on the node that you want to import the standard process flow into and select the **Import** option in the footer.

Importing Business Process Flows From Other Libraries

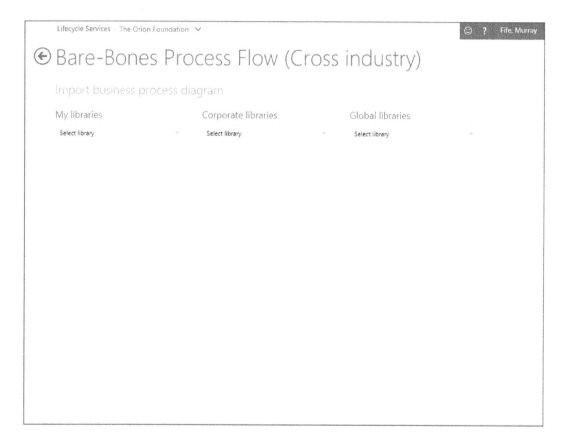

This will open up a search page showing you the different library types within Lifecycle Services.

Importing Business Process Flows From Other Libraries

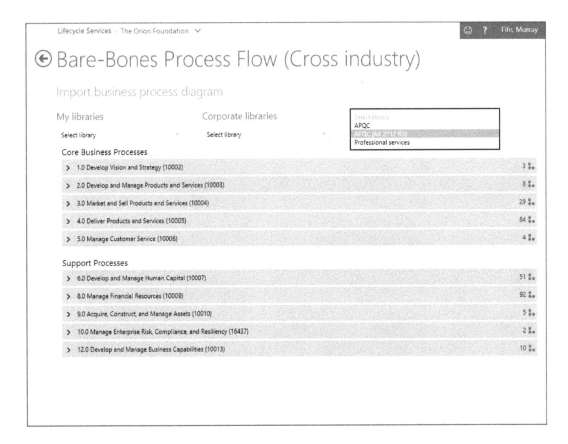

All you need to do is select the library that you want to import the model in from and you will see all of the steps within the body of the page.

Importing Business Process Flows From Other Libraries

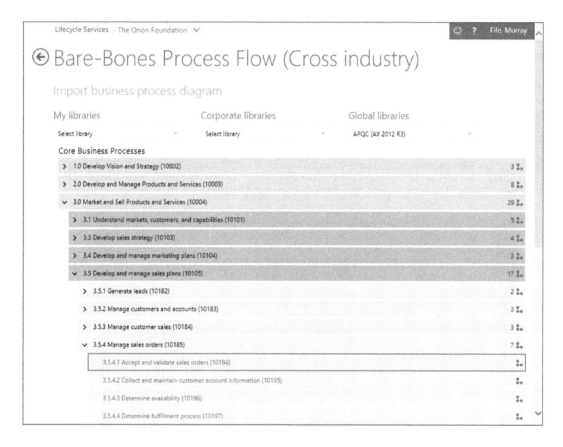

You can expand out all of the nodes until you get to the Business Process Flow that you want to use and then you just double click on it.

Importing Business Process Flows From Other Libraries

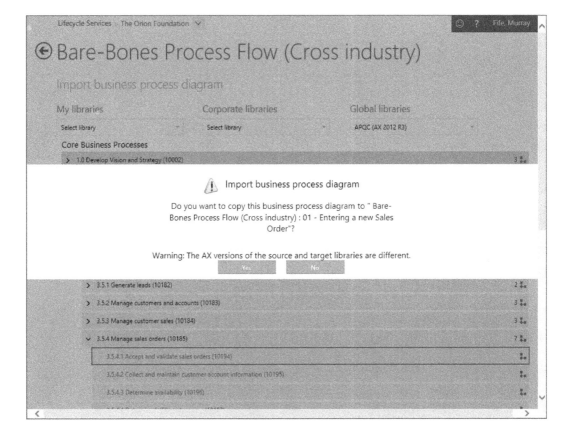

Lifecycle Services may warn you about version differences but you can throw caution to the wind and click the **Yes** button to import it.

Importing Business Process Flows From Other Libraries

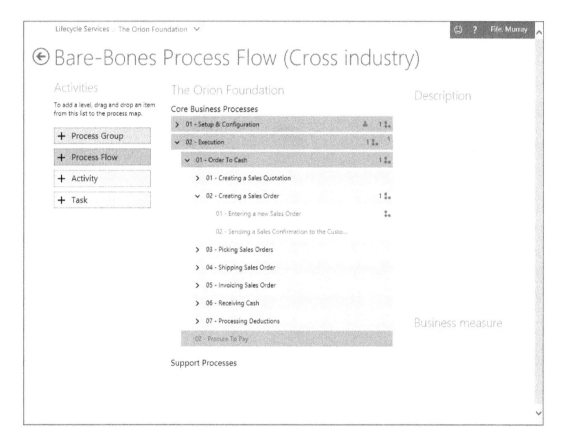

Now when you return to your **Business Process** you will see that you now have a business flow associated with it.

Importing Business Process Flows From Other Libraries

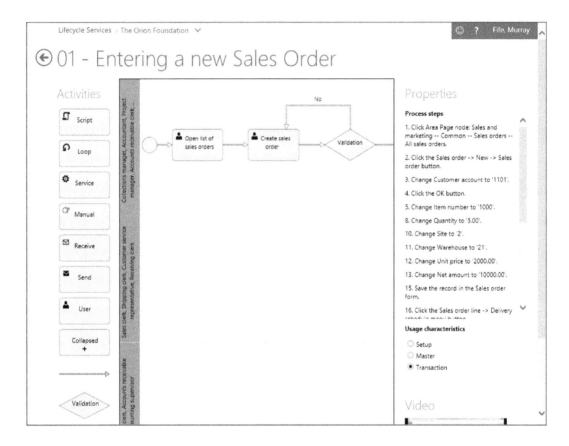

If you drill in you will see that all of the properties have been updated for the flow and also you have the standard video for the process flow as well.

It's not plagiarism, it's taking advantage of something that is already written.

ESTIMATING INFRASTRUCTURE REQUIREMENTS THROUGH LIFECYCLE SERVICES

One of the struggles within a Dynamics AX project has always been how many users do you need (and what types of users) and also how much hardware do we need to run the system. In the past it may have seemed like a little bit of Voodoo was used to calculate this information, but now with Lifecycle Services, you have the tools built in that will help you with all of these processes automatically with no black magic involved.

Estimating the User Licenses Using The License Estimator

Before you work out how much hardware you need, you need to start off by working out how many users you need on the system.

Estimating the User Licenses Using The License Estimator

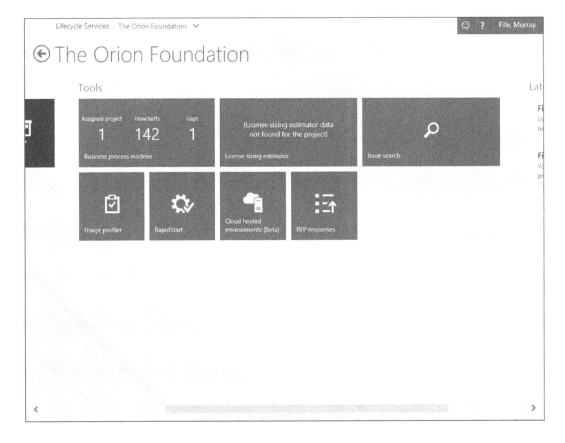

To do this, go to the Project home page and click on the **License Sizing Estimator** tile.

Estimating the User Licenses Using The License Estimator

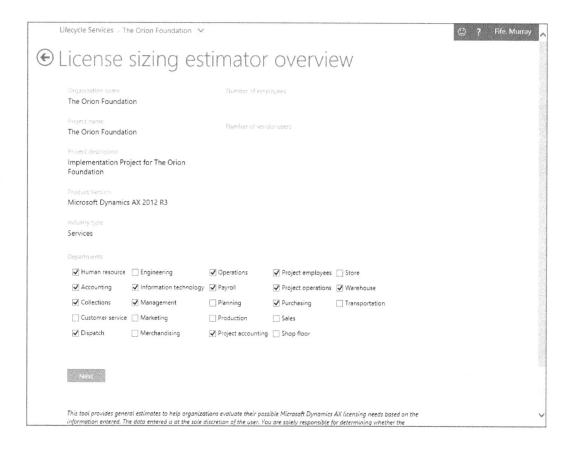

If this is the first time that you are using the **License Sizing Estimator** then it will ask you for some general user count and usage information.

Estimating the User Licenses Using The License Estimator

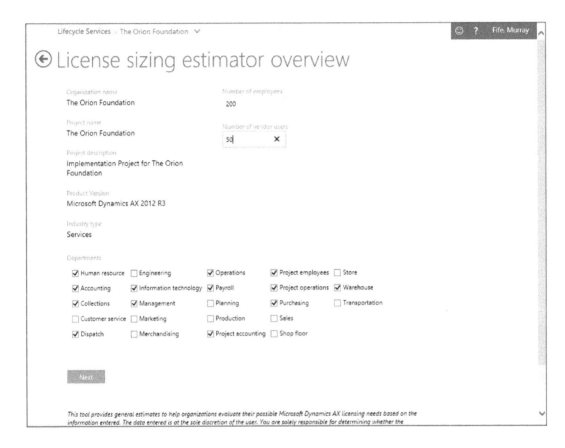

Just fill in the **Number of Employees**, the **Number of Vendor Users.**

Estimating the User Licenses Using The License Estimator

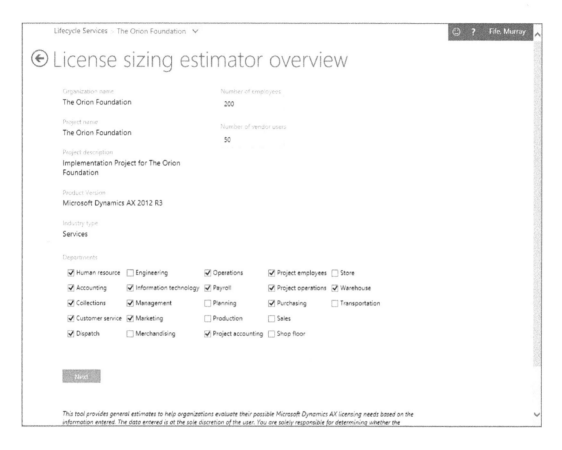

Then check (or uncheck) any departments that you will or will not be assigning users to.

Estimating the User Licenses Using The License Estimator

The Orion Foundation

50

Project description

Implementation of The Orion Foundation

Product Version

Microsoft Dynamics AX 2012 R3

Industry type

Services

Departments

☑ Human resource	☑ Engineering	☑ Operations	☑ Project employees	☐ Store
☑ Accounting	☑ Information technology	☑ Payroll	☑ Project operations	☑ Warehouse
☑ Collections	☑ Management	☐ Planning	☑ Purchasing	☐ Transportation
☑ Customer service	☑ Marketing	☐ Production	☑ Sales	
☑ Dispatch	☐ Merchandising	☑ Project accounting	☐ Shop floor	

Next

This tool provides general estimates to help organizations evaluate their possible Microsoft Dynamics AX licensing needs based on the information entered. The data entered is at the sole discretion of the user. You are solely responsible for determining whether the information is appropriate for your organization's business needs. Information obtained from this tool should not be considered an offer, a solicitation of an offer, or a recommendation by Microsoft for any licenses or subscriptions to Microsoft Dynamics software or services. Results are for general information only, provided "as is" and not warranted to be error-free. The estimator is not intended to serve as the primary or sole basis for an organization's licensing investment decision. You should not act (or refrain from acting) based on the information obtained from this tool without obtaining advice from your professional advisors about your organization's particular facts and circumstances.

When you have done that, just click on the **Next** button.

Estimating the User Licenses Using The License Estimator

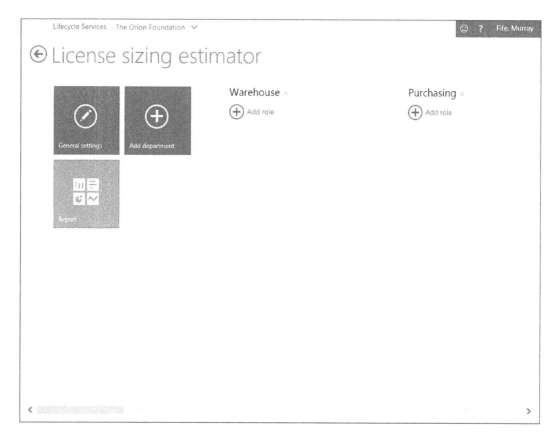

This will take you to the **License Sizing Estimator** worksheet.

Estimating the User Licenses Using The License Estimator

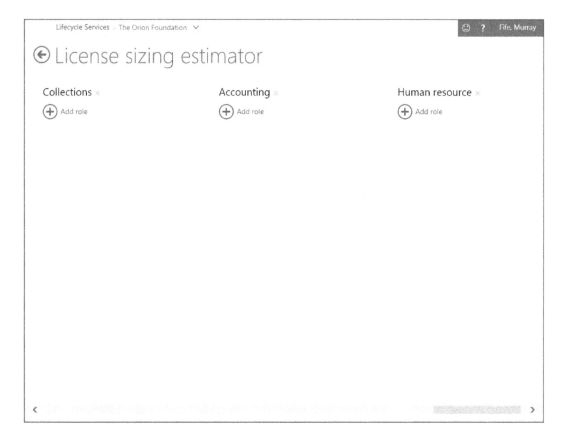

If you scroll to the right you will see that every **Department** that you selected will be listed there. To add a user role count to any of the departments, just click on the **Add Role** button.

Estimating the User Licenses Using The License Estimator

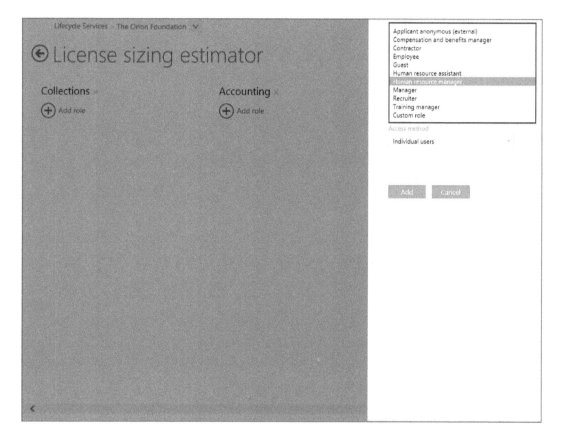

When the **Add Role** panel is displayed, you can select the particular **Role** from the dropdown list that is specific to the Department.

Estimating the User Licenses Using The License Estimator

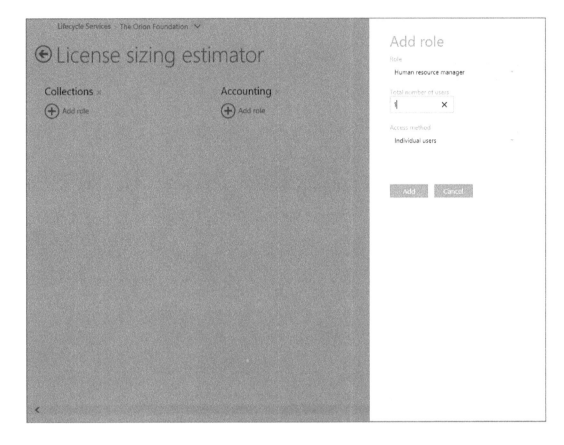

And then you can estimate the **Total Number of Users** that will be assigned to the Role.

When you are done, just click on the **Add** button.

Estimating the User Licenses Using The License Estimator

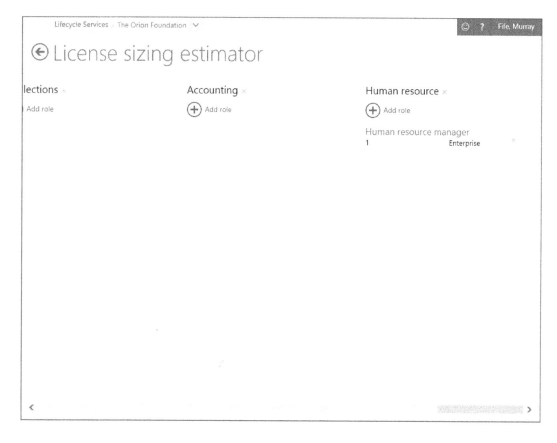

When you return to the **License Sizing Estimator** you will see that there is a new Role and it will also tell you the type of user license you need for that role (Enterprise, Functional, Task, or Self-service).

Estimating the User Licenses Using The License Estimator

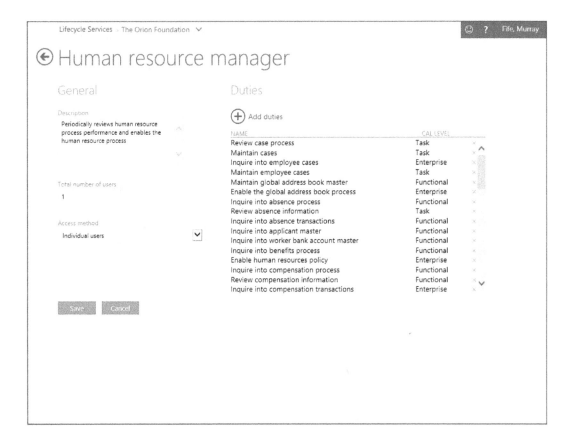

As a side note – if you click on the role, then you will see all of the duties associated with the role and if you want to tweak them then you can.

Estimating the User Licenses Using The License Estimator

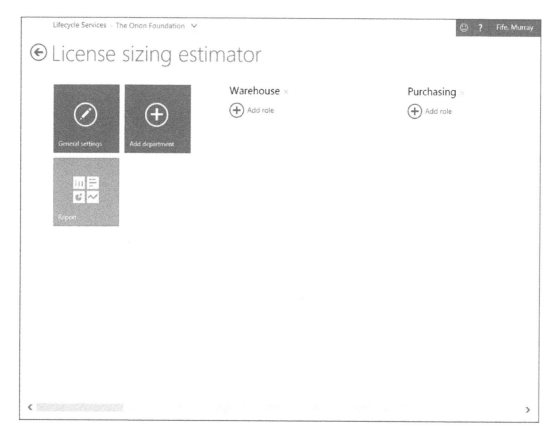

After you have finished adding all of your roles to the **License Sizing Estimator** then you can click on the **Report** tile.

Estimating the User Licenses Using The License Estimator

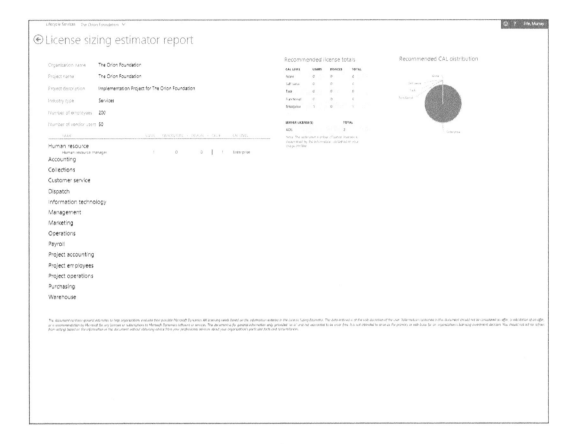

This will open up a report that shows you a breakdown of all the users that are required from a licensing standpoint.

Estimating the User Licenses Using The License Estimator

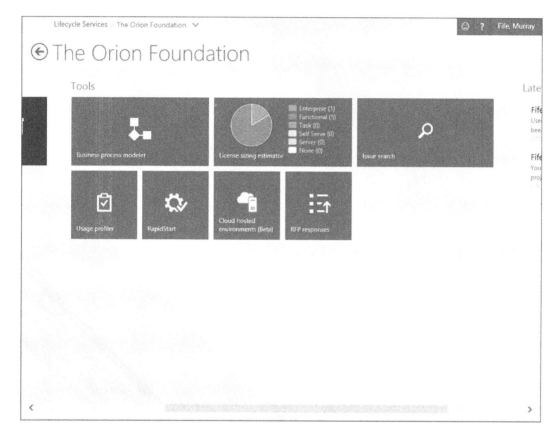

Also, when you return to the **Project** dashboard you will see all of the user counts are summarized there as well on the **Licensing Sizing Estimator** tile.

Adding New Departments To The Licensing Estimator

Although there are a lot of different departments that are already pre-configured within Lifecycle Services, sometimes there may be unique departments that don't quite fit into the standard mold within the project. Not a problem – you can create your own custom departments.

Adding New Departments To The Licensing Estimator

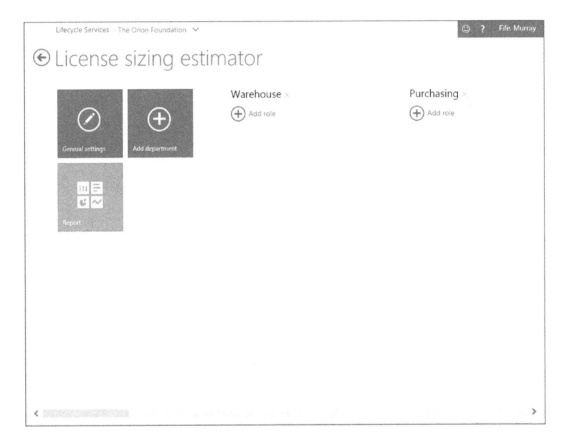

To do this, just click on the **Add Department** tile within the **License Sizing Estimator** page.

Adding New Departments To The Licensing Estimator

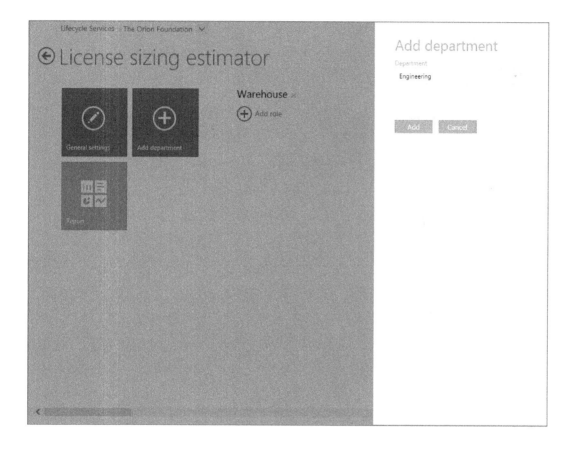

Adding New Departments To The Licensing Estimator

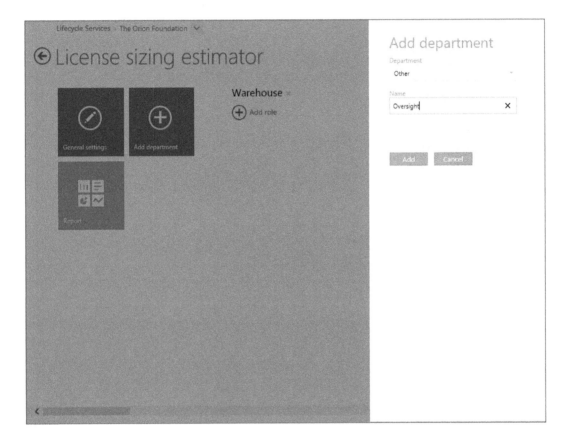

When the **Add Department** panel is displayed, click on the **Department** dropdown and select the **Other** option. This will allow you to type in a custom Department **Name**.

When you are done, just click on the **Add** button.

Adding New Departments To The Licensing Estimator

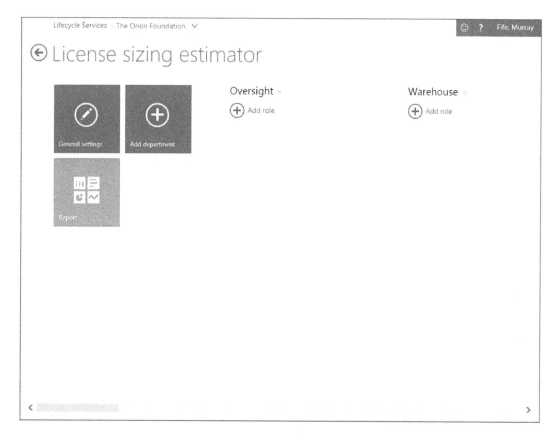

When you return back to the **License Sizing Estimator** you will see that there is a new **Department** column for your new custom department.

Adding Custom Roles To The Licensing Estimator

In addition to Departments, there are probably roles within the organization that don't quite fit into the ones that are initially delivered within Lifecycle Services. Don't worry about this either, you can create your own custom Roles on the fly and also have Lifecycle Services help you with the type of user license that is required for the user.

Adding Custom Roles To The Licensing Estimator

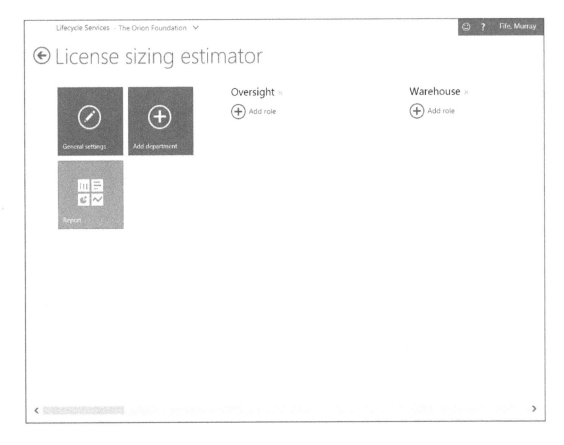

To do this, click on the **Add Role** button under the Department that you want to add the role to.

Adding Custom Roles To The Licensing Estimator

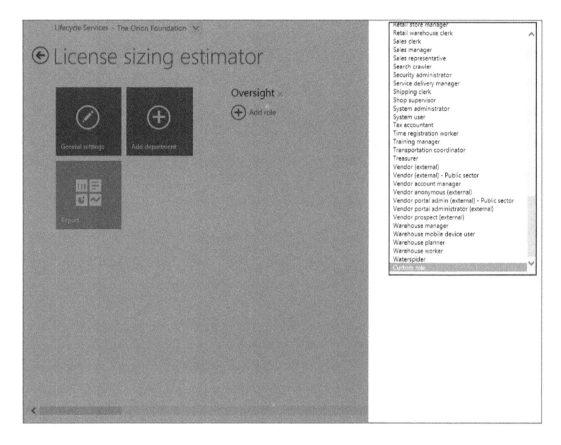

When the **Add Role** panel is displayed, you will be able to select from any of the pre-configured roles or select a **Custom Role**.

Adding Custom Roles To The Licensing Estimator

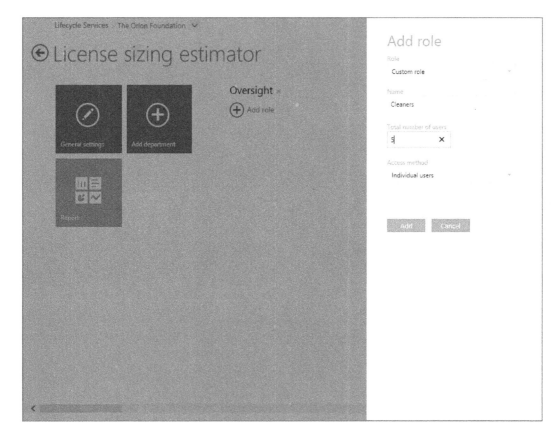

This will allow you to create a new Role **Name** and also specify the number of users before clicking on the **Add** button.

Adding Custom Roles To The Licensing Estimator

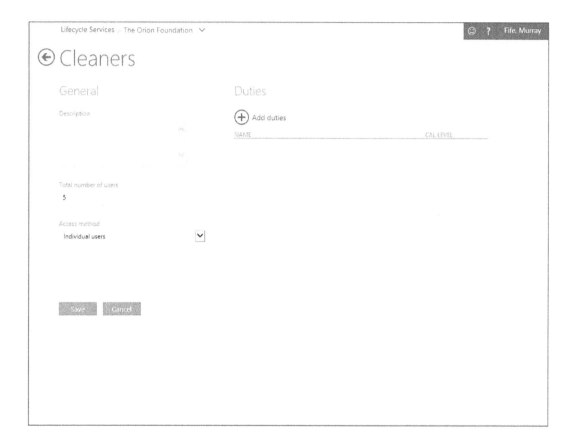

Since this is a custom Role, there is a little bit of extra work to do because Lifecycle Services doesn't know what type of user this is, and will take you straight to the roles details. To configure the Role, click on the **Add Duties** button under the **Duties** group.

Adding Custom Roles To The Licensing Estimator

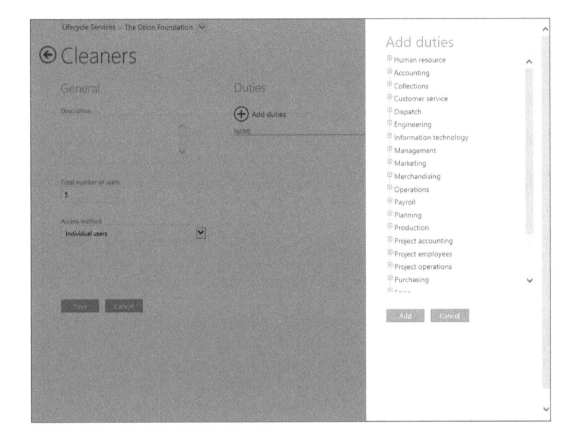

This will open up a **Add Duties** panel.

Adding Custom Roles To The Licensing Estimator

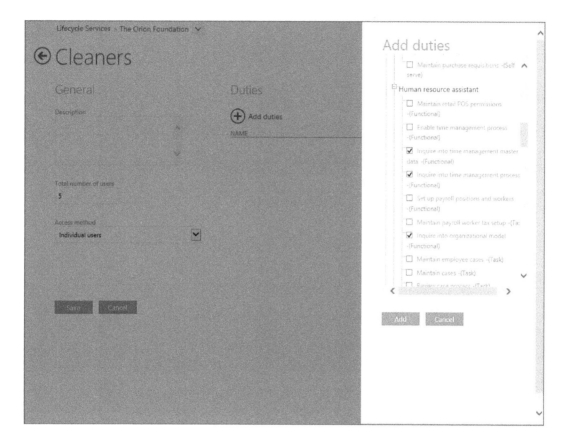

All you need to do is select the Duties from the list and then click on the **Add** button.

Adding Custom Roles To The Licensing Estimator

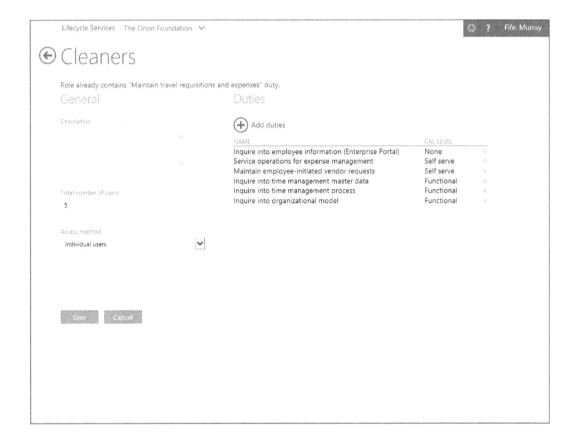

When you return to the roles details you will notice that all of the duties are listed, along with the CAL license required for them.

When you are done configuring the role, just click on the **Save** button.

Adding Custom Roles To The Licensing Estimator

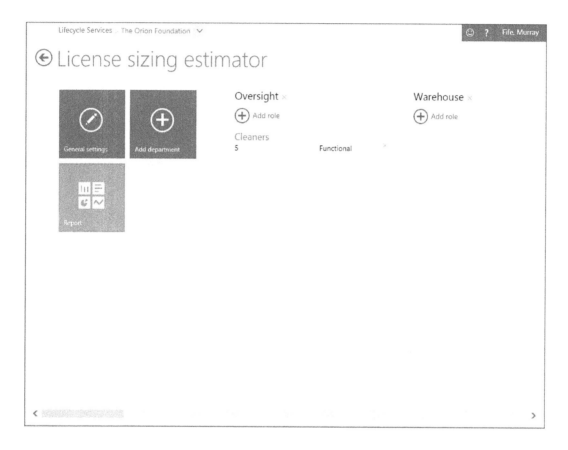

When you return to the **License Sizing Estimator** page you will be able to see your new custom role, along with the type of user license that is required for it.

Estimating Hardware Requirements Using The Lifecycle Services Usage Profiler

Lifecycle Services has a nifty feature that allows you to estimate your hardware requirements based on your business process flows and also your expected transactional usage within the system. This is a great way to get the official sizing's for your Dynamics AX system directly from the source – Microsoft.

This will ensure that you don't create a system that is either under or over powered.

Estimating Hardware Requirements Using The Lifecycle Services Usage Profiler

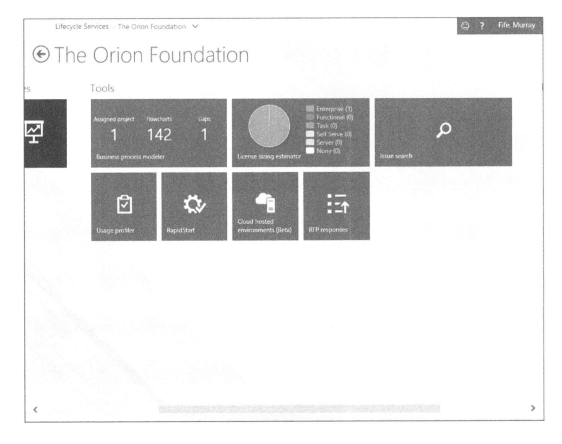

Start off by opening up your project within Lifecycle Services and clicking on the **Usage Profiler** tile.

Estimating Hardware Requirements Using The Lifecycle Services Usage Profiler

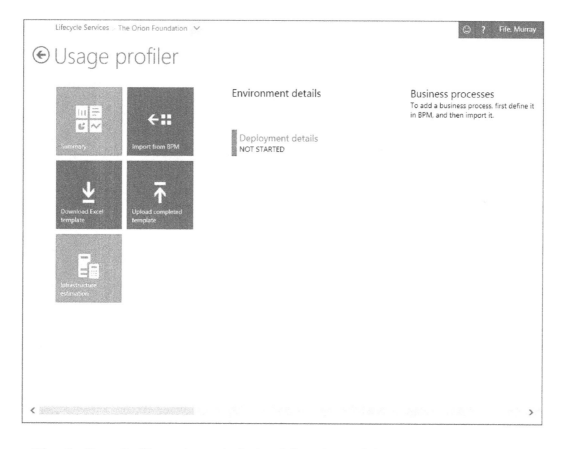

When the **Usage Profiler** workspace is displayed, if you have existing Business Processes within your project, click on the **Import from BPM** tile.

Estimating Hardware Requirements Using The Lifecycle Services Usage Profiler

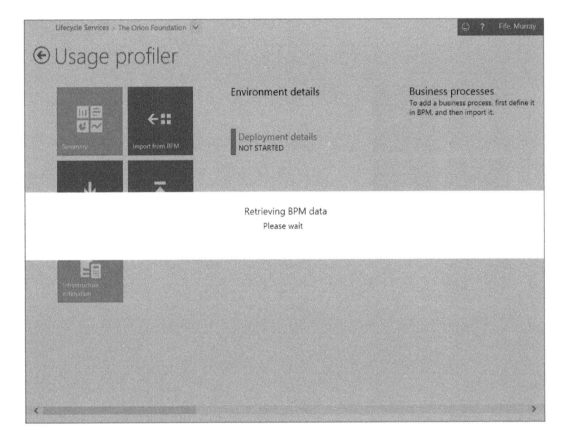

This will grab all of your existing Business Process models and integrate them in with the usage data.

Estimating Hardware Requirements Using The Lifecycle Services Usage Profiler

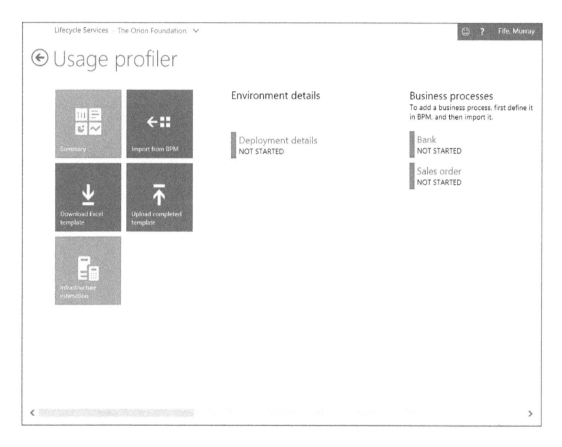

After the import is complete then you will see the areas that you will be using within the **Business Process** column.

Estimating Hardware Requirements Using The Lifecycle Services Usage Profiler

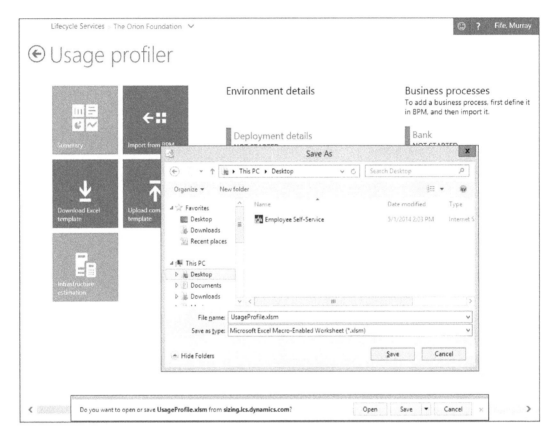

Now click on the **Download Excel Template** tile and save the Excel workbook that it creates for you.

Estimating Hardware Requirements Using The Lifecycle Services Usage Profiler

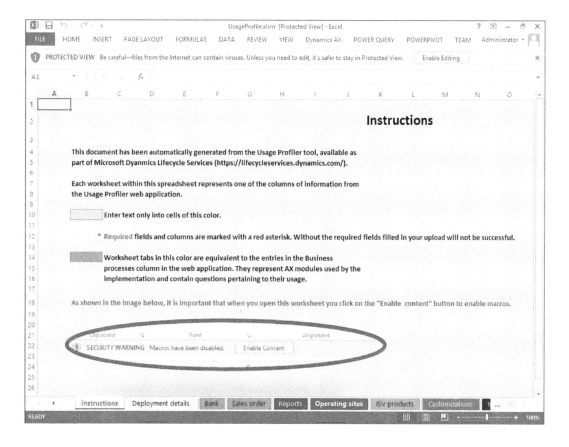

When you open up the workbook, click on the **Enable Editing** button to enable the content.

Estimating Hardware Requirements Using The Lifecycle Services Usage Profiler

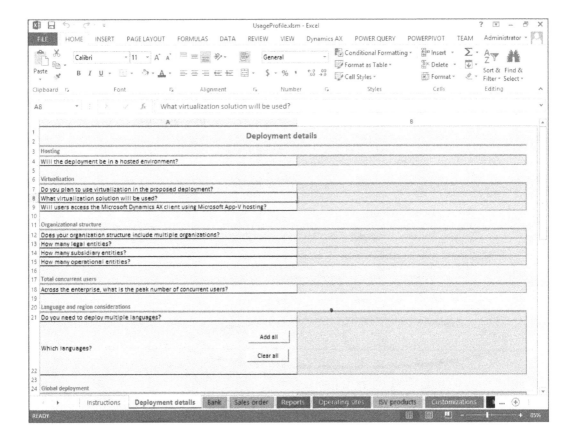

Now switch to the **Deployment Details** and you will see that there are a number of questions for you to answer based on your expected deployment profile.

Estimating Hardware Requirements Using The Lifecycle Services Usage Profiler

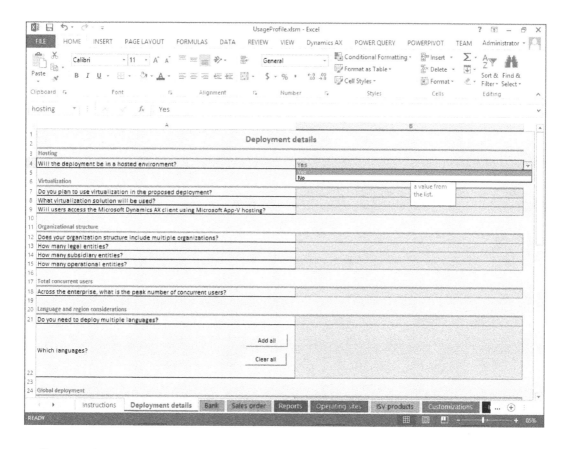

All you need to do is click on the dropdown and select the appropriate answer.

Estimating Hardware Requirements Using The Lifecycle Services Usage Profiler

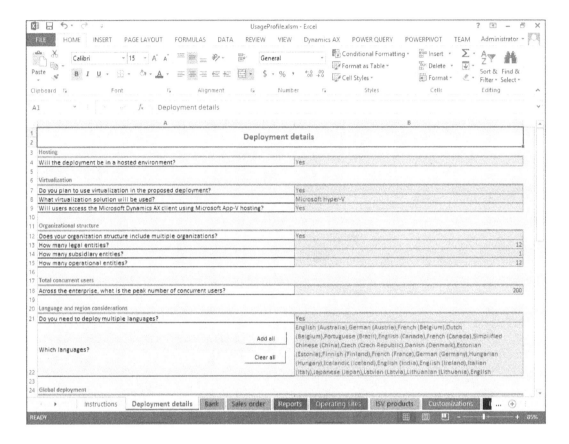

Now just Answer as many of the questions as you can.

Estimating Hardware Requirements Using The Lifecycle Services Usage Profiler

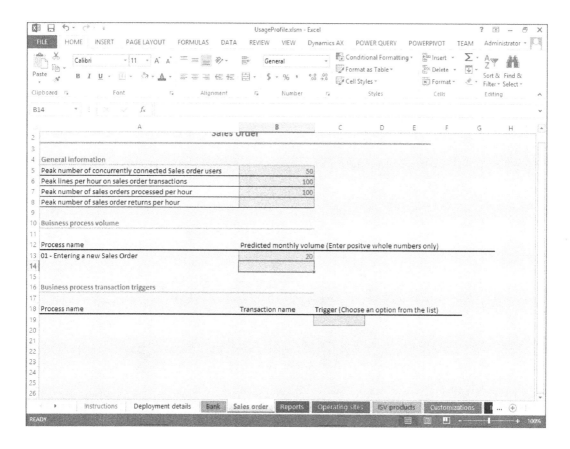

If you imported any Business Process Models, then you will also notice that there are tabs for all of the other functional areas like Sales etc. If you want to update those details with the transaction volumes, then this will help LCS size your hardware appropriately.

Estimating Hardware Requirements Using The Lifecycle Services Usage Profiler

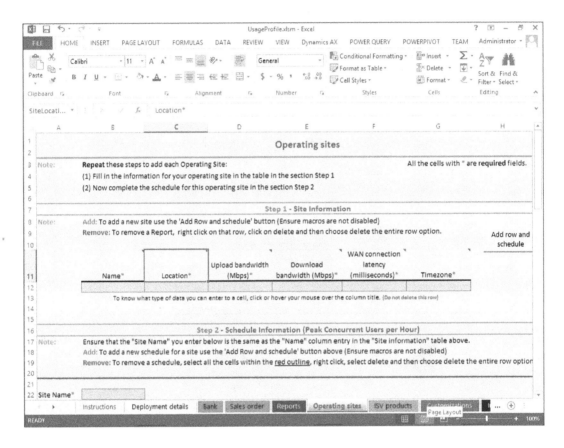

If you really want to get detailed then you can also enter in all of your organizational profiles as well within the **Operating Sites** tabs.

After you have updated as much as you can, just save and close the Workbook.

Estimating Hardware Requirements Using The Lifecycle Services Usage Profiler

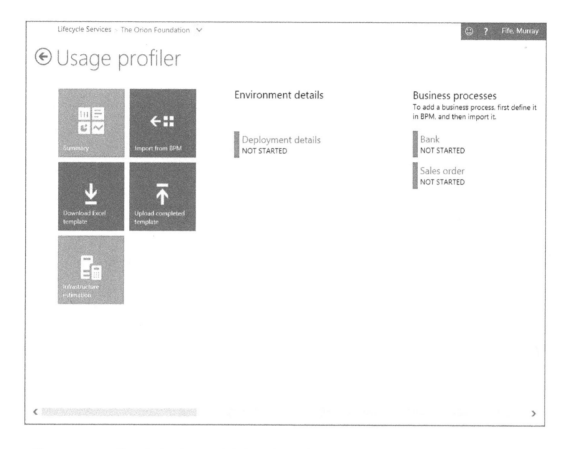

Now return to Lifecycle Services and click on the **Upload Completed Template** tile.

Estimating Hardware Requirements Using The Lifecycle Services Usage Profiler

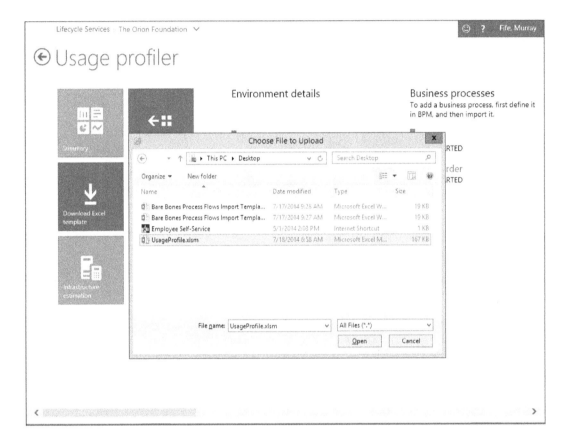

Find the completed spreadsheet and then click on the **Open** button.

Estimating Hardware Requirements Using The Lifecycle Services Usage Profiler

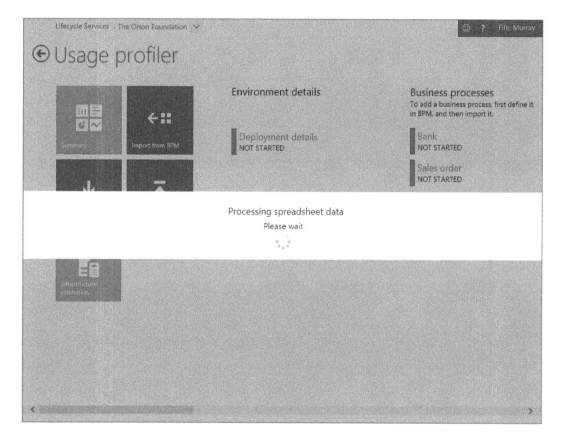

Lifecycle Services will then take all of your profile data and process for a little bit.

Estimating Hardware Requirements Using The Lifecycle Services Usage Profiler

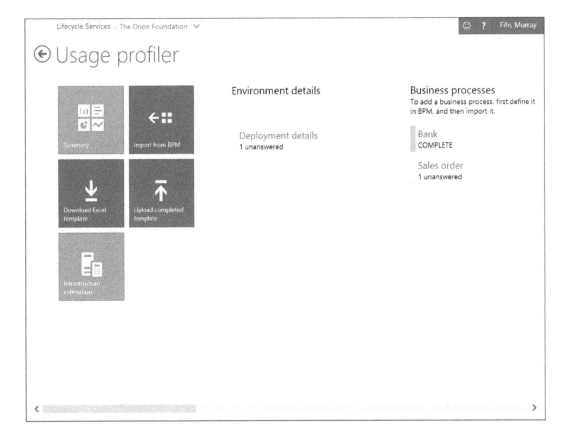

Now you will see that the **Environment Details** and the **Business Processes** columns will be updated with different statuses. If you have questions that have not been completed, then just click on the tile.

Estimating Hardware Requirements Using The Lifecycle Services Usage Profiler

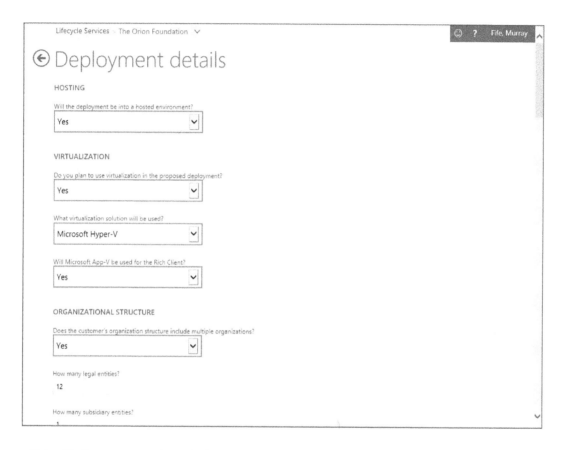

This will allow you to update all of the information that was on the spreadsheet on-line.

Estimating Hardware Requirements Using The Lifecycle Services Usage Profiler

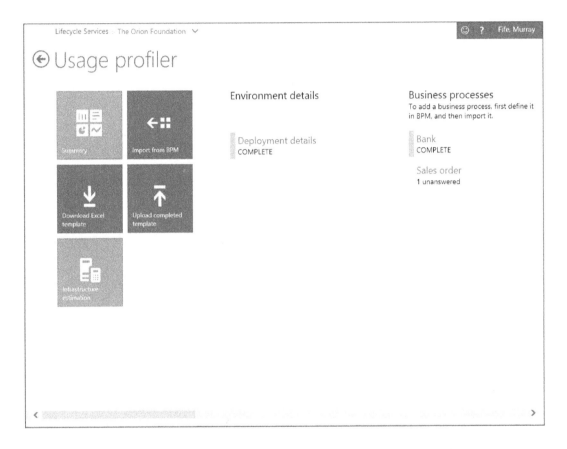

Once you have completed as much as you can within the Usage Profile, just click on the **Infrastructure Estimation** tile.

Estimating Hardware Requirements Using The Lifecycle Services Usage Profiler

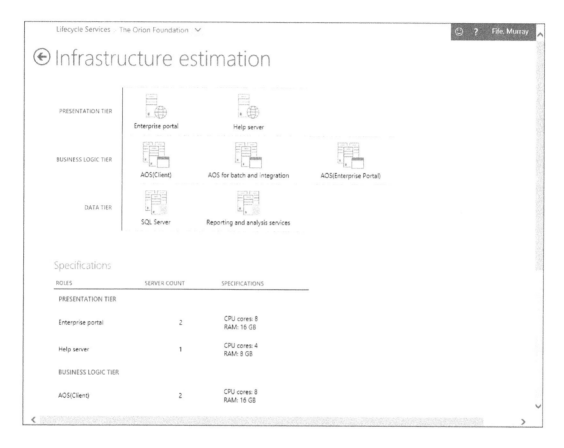

Lifecycle Services will give you a breakdown of all the hardware and configuration profiles so that you can start estimating your hardware and hosting costs.

How easy is that!

TRACKING PROJECT DETAILS THROUGH LIFECYCLE SERVICES

One of the reasons why Lifecycle Services is so important is that it gives you one place to manage all to the activities associated with the implementation and care of the Dynamics AX projects and implementations. One important piece of this is the project management aspect, and there are a number of tools that are available in the service that help you with this as well.

In this chapter we will look at the Project Management capabilities that are built into the Lifecycle Services system.

Modifying Business Process Flows And Creating Gap Lists

If the Business Process Models that are created by the Task Recorder don't quite match up with how you really want to do business, or if there are additional steps that you want to add to your Business Process Models that were not included in the Task Recording, then that's not a problem. Lifecycle Services allows you wo update your Business Process Models after they have been uploaded and it will also track the changes that you make and add them to a automatically created Gap List.

Modifying Business Process Flows And Creating Gap Lists

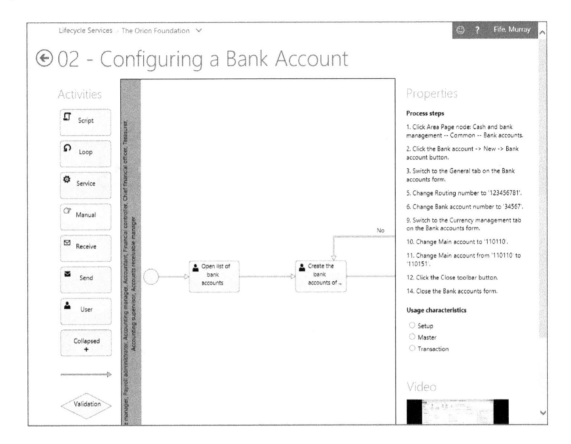

To see this in action, just open up one of your Business Process Models.

Modifying Business Process Flows And Creating Gap Lists

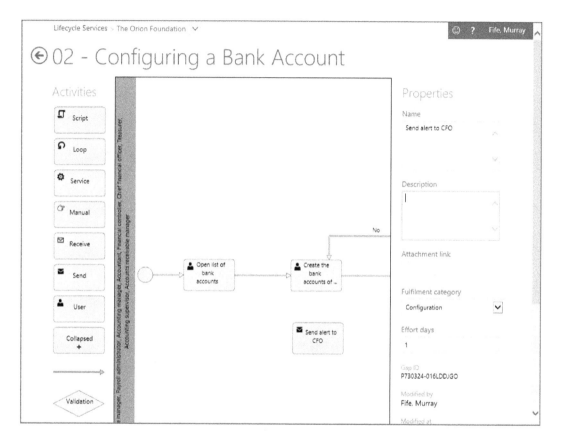

Now drag and drop any of the Business Process **Activities** from the left hand side of the page onto the Model canvas. When you do this you will notice that you can update the **Name** and **Description** for the step.

Modifying Business Process Flows And Creating Gap Lists

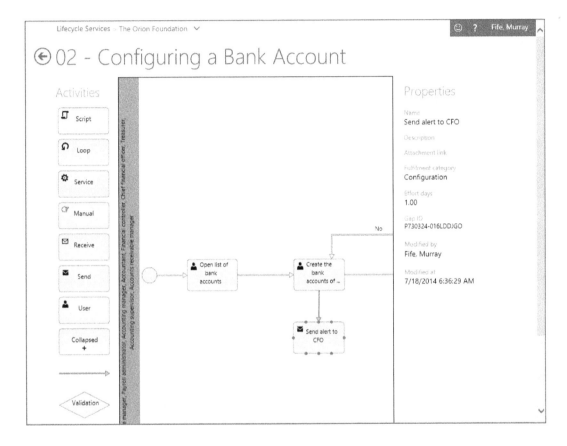

If you drag an arrow over onto the canvas and drop it onto the starting node, then you will be able to also link it with other nodes in the Business Process Model.

Modifying Business Process Flows And Creating Gap Lists

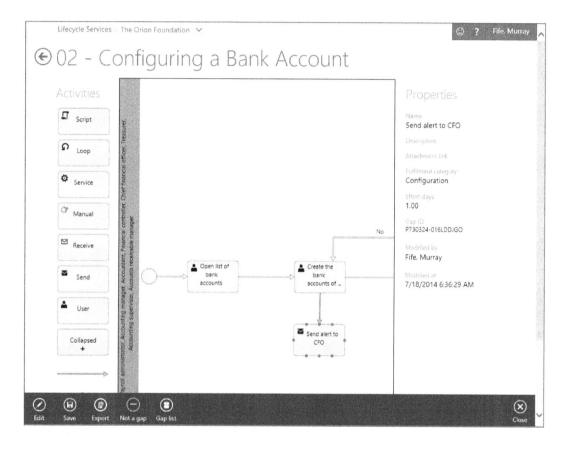

When you are done with your changes, right-mouse-click on the canvas to open up the actions panel at the bottom of the page and select the **Save** option to save the changes.

After you have done that, right-mouse-click again and click on the **Gap List** button.

Modifying Business Process Flows And Creating Gap Lists

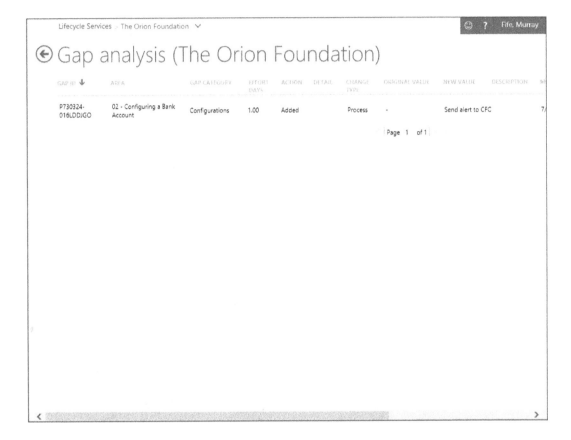

This will open up a Gap Analysis page and show you all of the changes that need to be made because of deviations from the standard Business Process Models.

Now this will make project management so much easier.

Adding Work Estimates to Business Process Flow Steps

There is another nifty feature within the Business Process Flows modelling tool that allows you to add work estimates the expected work required to complete a task.

Adding Work Estimates to Business Process Flow Steps

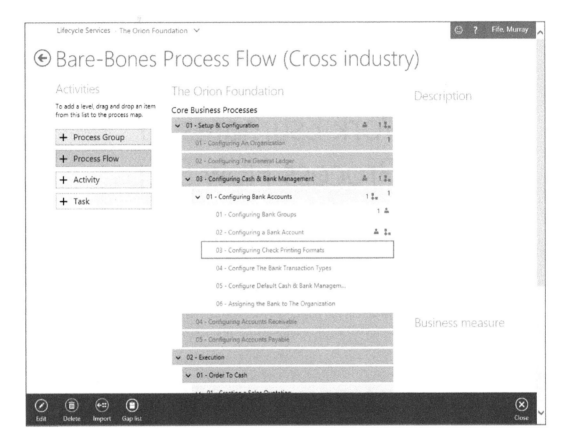

To do this, open up your Business Process Flow, right-mouse-click on the process node that you want to add estimates to and then click on the **Edit** button.

Adding Work Estimates to Business Process Flow Steps

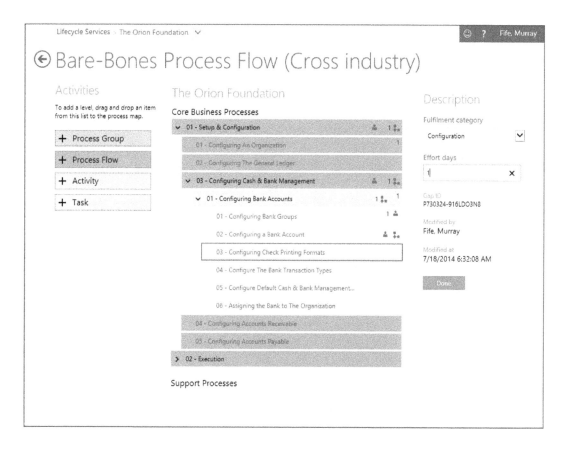

This will allow you to update the properties of the step, and also update the **Effort Days** field.

Adding Work Estimates to Business Process Flow Steps

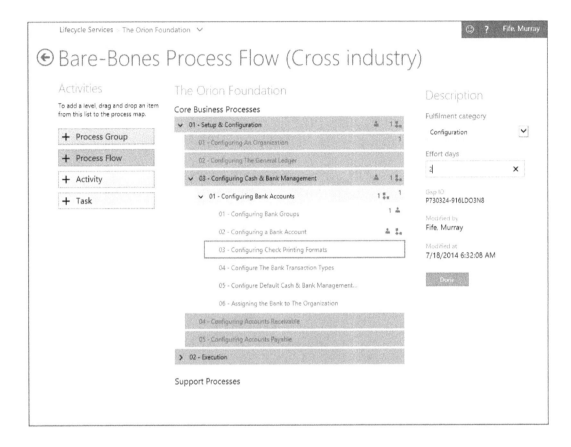

All you need to do is change the **Effort Days** and then click on the **Done** button to save it back to the Business Process Flow.

Adding Work Estimates to Business Process Flow Steps

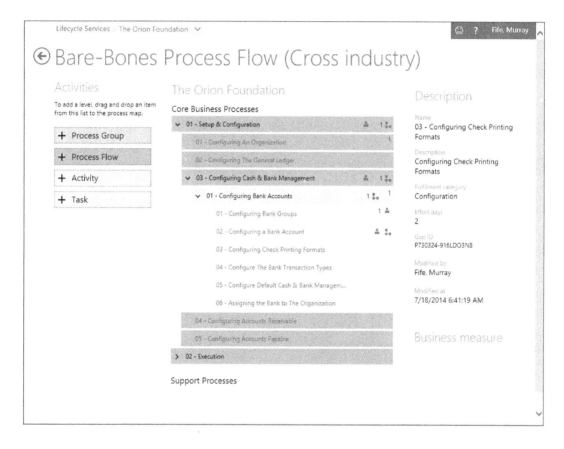

This will also roll up to the parent level as well showing you the total effort at the parent levels as well.

Creating Business Process Documentation From Process Flows

There is another self documenting option available within the Lifecycle Services portal as well that allows you to create project documentation for entire Business Processes.

Creating Business Process Documentation From Process Flows

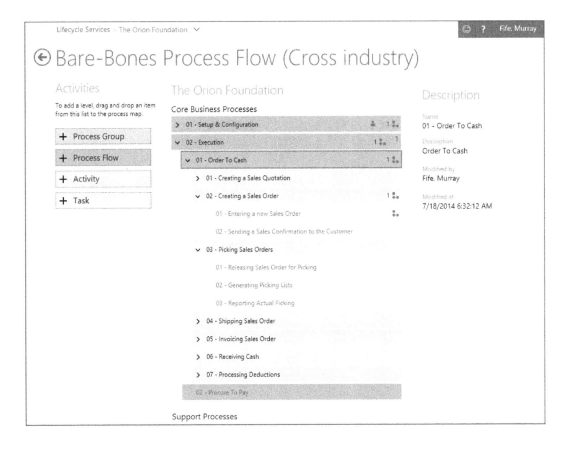

To do this, start off by opening up your Business Process Flow.

Creating Business Process Documentation From Process Flows

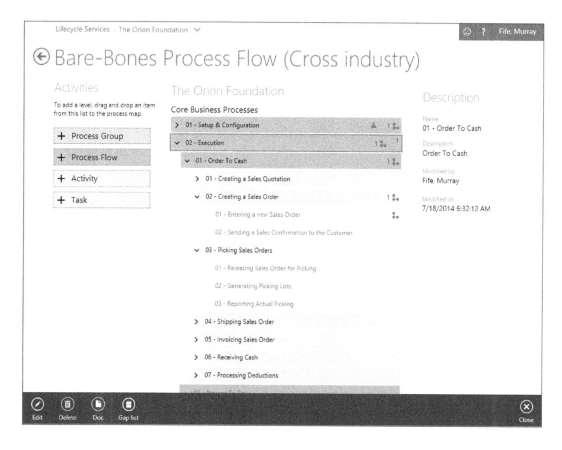

Then right-mouse-click on a parent node and select the **Doc** menu item that is shown in the footer.

Creating Business Process Documentation From Process Flows

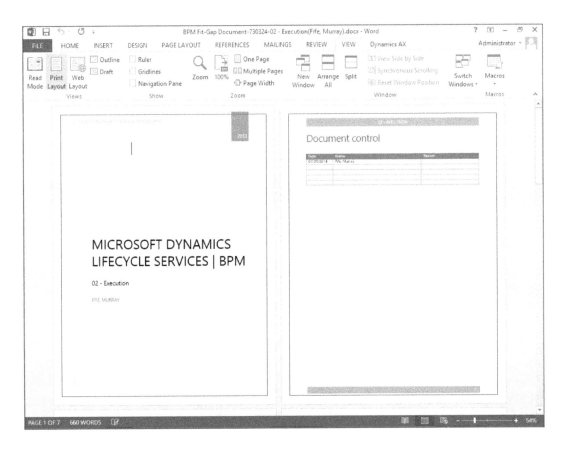

Lifecycle Services will crank away for a little bit and you will end up with a Word document that describes all of the Business Processes in detail.

It's almost like it's doing all of the menial project work for you.

Tracking Issues against the Project

Another Project Management tool that is embedded within Lifecycle services is the ability to track project **Issues** – i.e. the things that pop up during the project that are not directly related to the business process flows. This gives you a single location where all of the project members can see the open issues and update their statuses.

Tracking Issues against the Project

To create an Issue, just click on the **Add Issue** button on the **Issues** tile within the **Project** group.

Tracking Issues against the Project

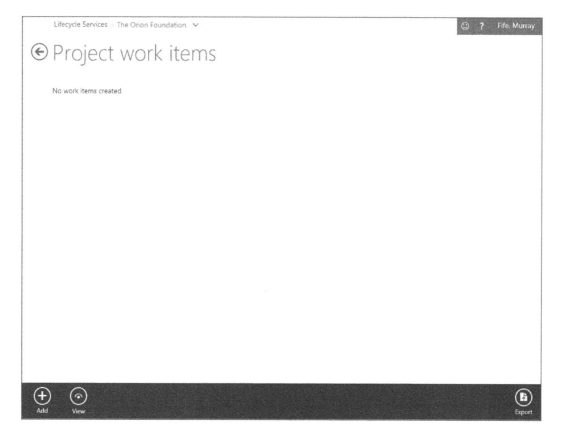

This will take you to the **Project Work Items** page. To create an issue, click on the **Add** button in the footer of the page.

Tracking Issues against the Project

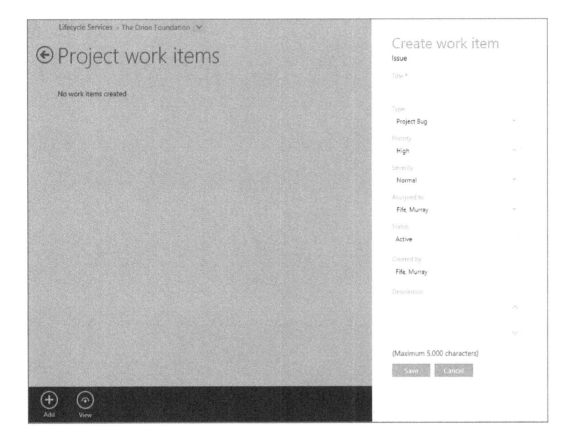

This will open up the **Create Work Item** panel with all the required fields for the issue.

Tracking Issues against the Project

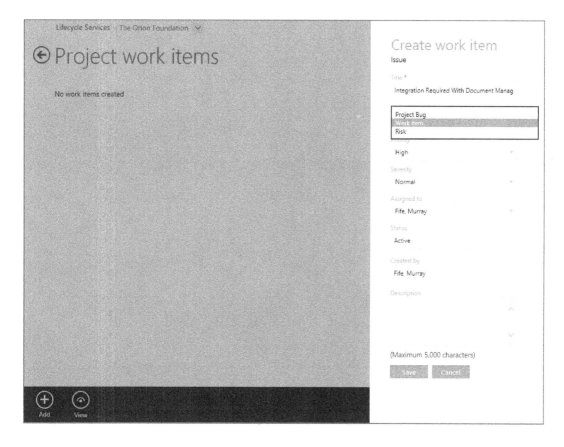

Assign the issue a **Title** and then select he **Issue Type** from the dropdown.

Tracking Issues against the Project

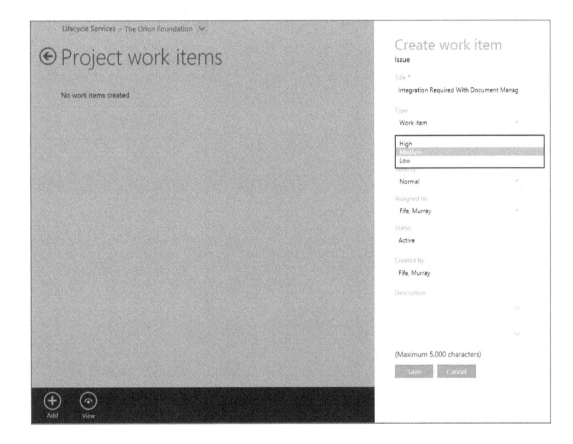

Then set the **Priority** of the issue.

Tracking Issues against the Project

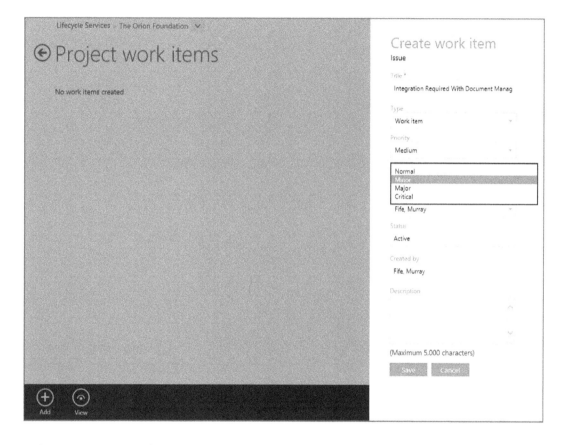

Choose the **Severity** of the issue.

Tracking Issues against the Project

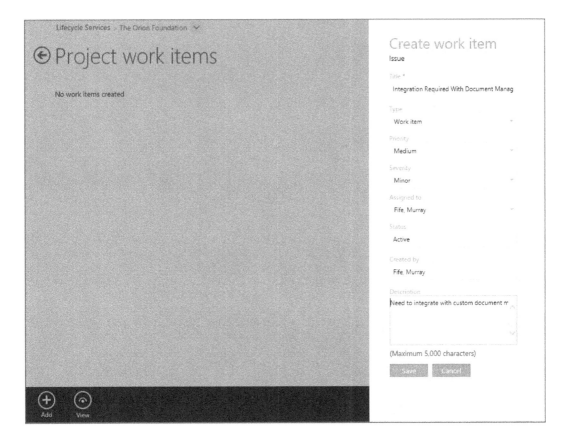

And then enter in any description that you want to associate with the issue.

When you are done, just click the **Save** button.

Tracking Issues against the Project

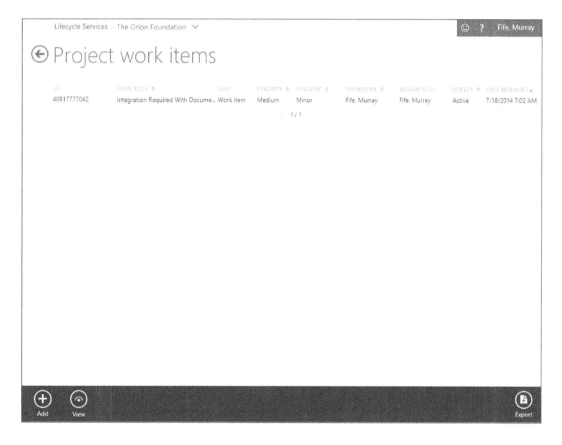

Now when you return to the **Project Work Items** page you will see that there is a new Issue recorded against the project.

If you want to export the Issue list to Excel than just click on the **Export** button in the bottom right of the form.

Tracking Issues against the Project

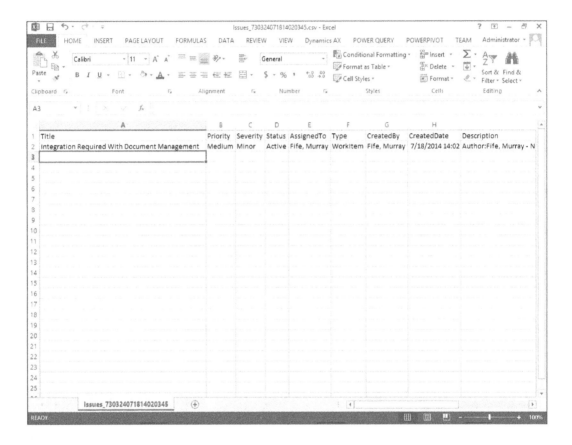

This will open up an Excel spreadsheet and you will see all of the Issues listed out.

Tracking Issues against the Project

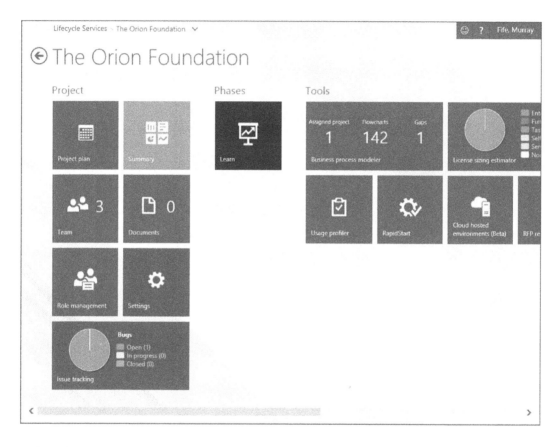

Also when you return to the **Project** home page you will see a summary of the Issues and also all of the statuses within the **Issues** tile.

Tracking Customizations

If you are using Lifecycle Services to manage an **Implementation** project type, then there are a few additional features that are available for that lifecycle phase. One of these is the feature that allows you to track and manage **Customizations** that you make to the system.

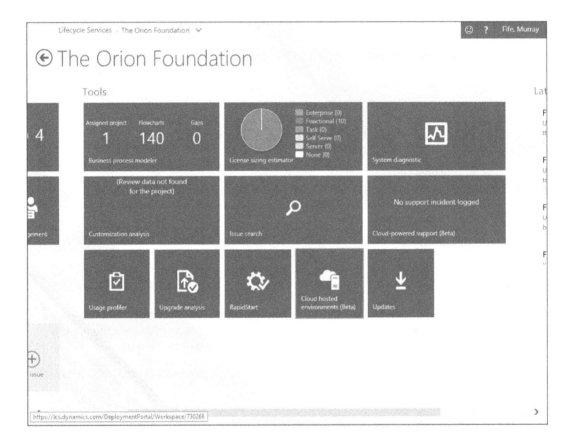

To record and track a new **Customization**, click on the **Customization Analysis** tile within the **Tools** group for your project.

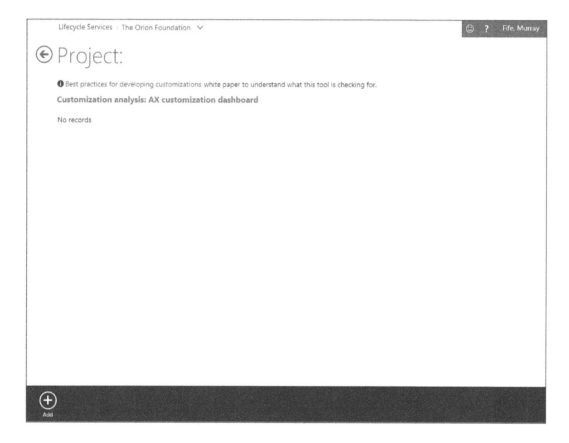

This will open up the Customization list page. To add a new Customization, click on the **Add** button in the footer of the page.

This will open up a new **Customization** details page.

Just fill out the Customization **Name** and **Description** and then click the **Create** button.

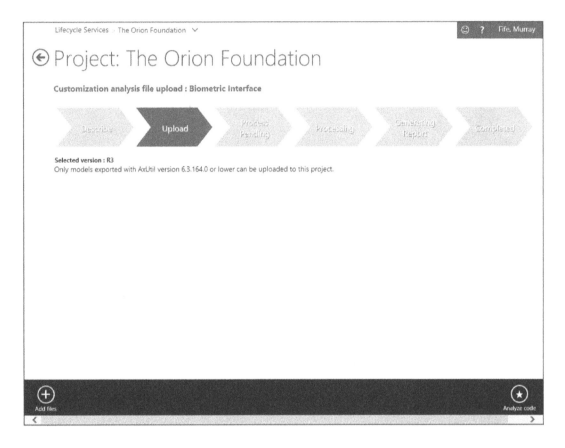

Once you have created the **Customization** record then it will start to move through the Customization flow and you will have more control over the management of the code and also be able to have Lifecycle Services analyze the code for you.

When you return to the **Customization List Page** you will get an overview of all the customizations in process.

This is looking like a well run project for sure.

Attach OneDrive Documents To Business Process Models Within Lifecycle Services

Lifecycle Services is the backbone to your Dynamics AX implementation since it allows you to model all of your business processes, and also track any changes that you may be making as you are getting up and running. It also has an option to attach documents to your projects and business process models. But the documents are stored within Lifecycle Services as links, and not as uploaded documents - probably because Microsoft doesn't want you filling up LCS with attachments. That's not a problem though because if you use OneDrive as your document filing system, then you can easily link them into your LCS projects and everyone has access to them without a problem.

Gone are the days of transporting documents around in your head...

Attach OneDrive Documents To Business Process Models Within Lifecycle Services

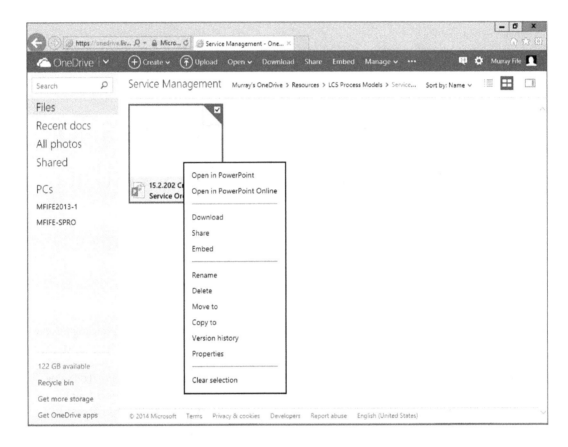

First we need to create a shared URL that we will point to within Lifecycle Services. To do this, open up **OneDrive** right-mouse-click on the document that you want to share and select the **Share** menu item.

Attach OneDrive Documents To Business Process Models Within Lifecycle Services

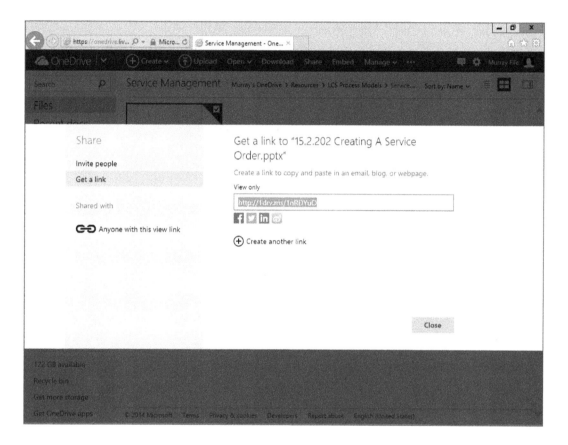

When the **Sharing** form is displayed, create a link (Read Only or Editable) and then note down the URL of the file.

Attach OneDrive Documents To Business Process Models Within Lifecycle Services

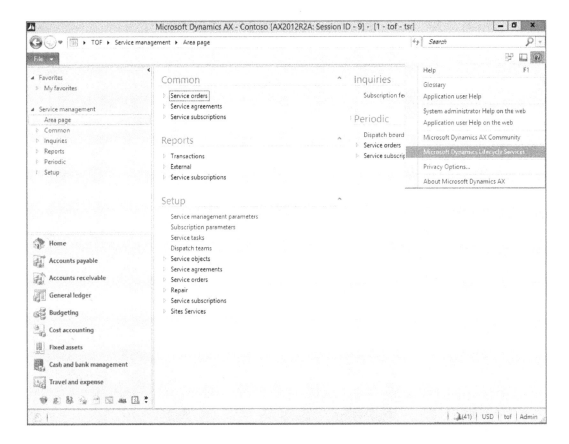

Now open up Lifecycle Services. With the R3 release of Dynamics AX you can now do this directly from the help menu.

Attach OneDrive Documents To Business Process Models Within Lifecycle Services

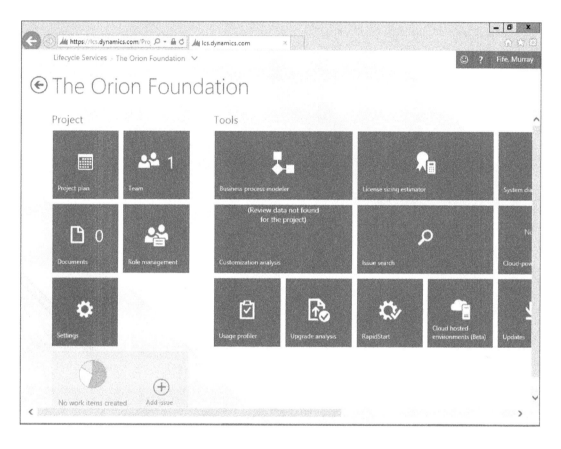

To attach a document to the project itself browse to your project and click on the **Documents** tile.

Attach OneDrive Documents To Business Process Models Within Lifecycle Services

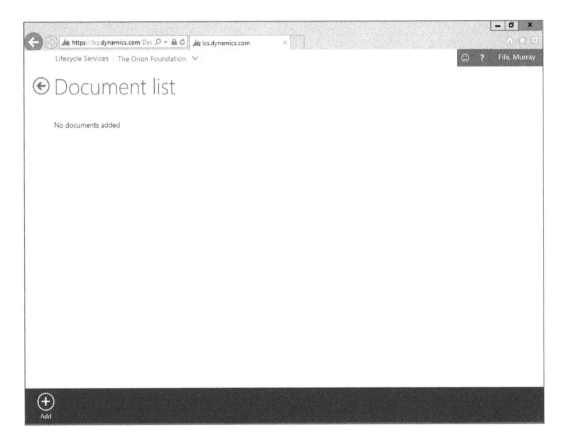

When the **Documents List** is displayed, click on the **Add** button in the footer of the site.

Attach OneDrive Documents To Business Process Models Within Lifecycle Services

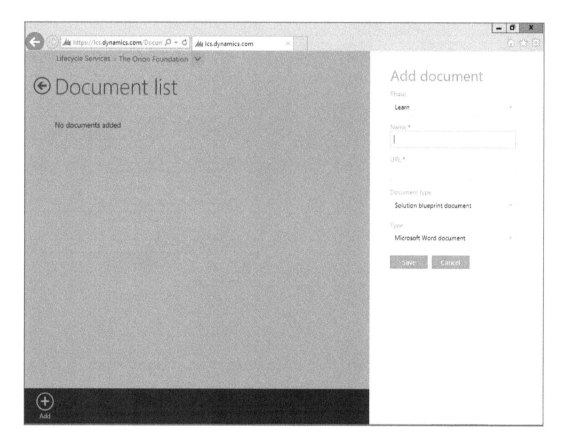

This will open up a **Add Document** panel.

Attach OneDrive Documents To Business Process Models Within Lifecycle Services

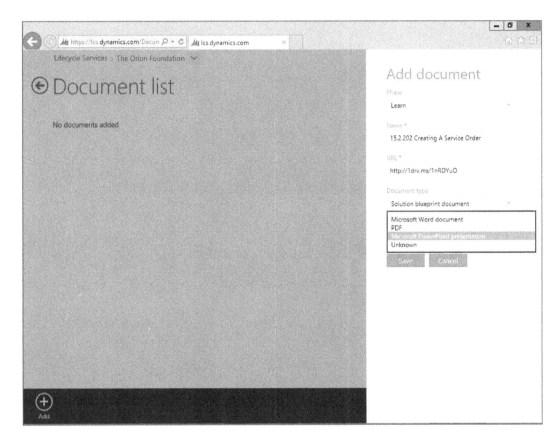

Now you can give your document a name, paste in the **URL** for the OneDrive document, and then also select the **Document Type**.

Attach OneDrive Documents To Business Process Models Within Lifecycle Services

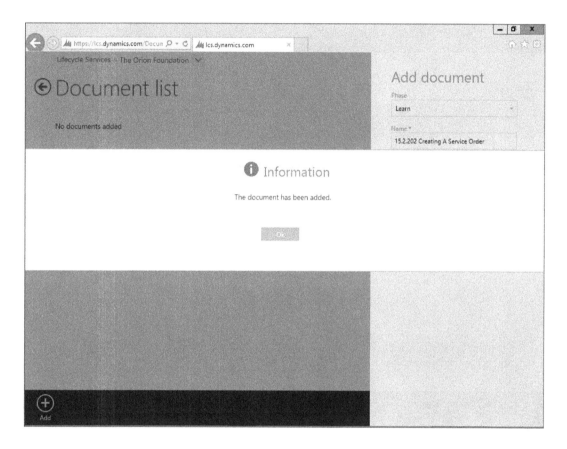

Then you can save the document link to Lifecycle Services.

Attach OneDrive Documents To Business Process Models Within Lifecycle Services

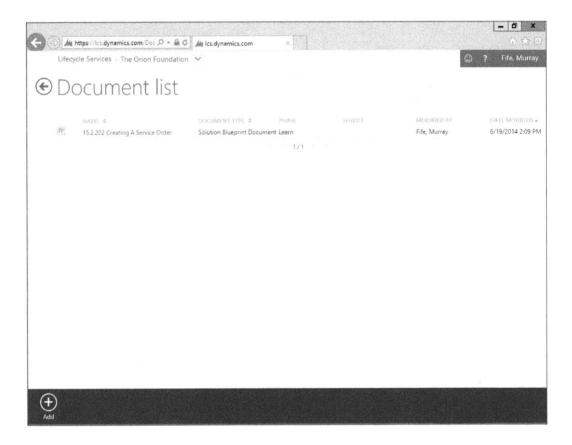

When you look at the **Document List** now you will see that the document is there for everyone to access.

Attach OneDrive Documents To Business Process Models Within Lifecycle Services

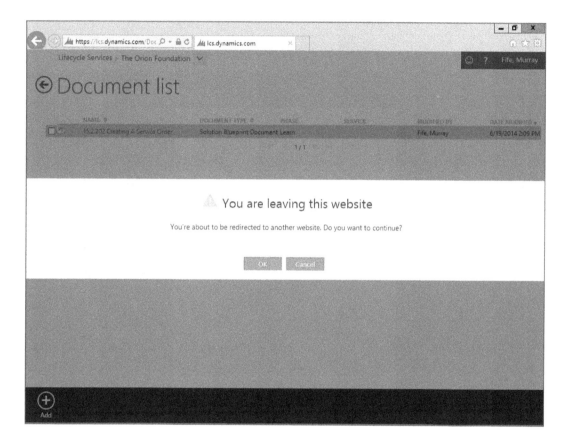

If you click on the link then you will be taken from LCS to the document.

Attach OneDrive Documents To Business Process Models Within Lifecycle Services

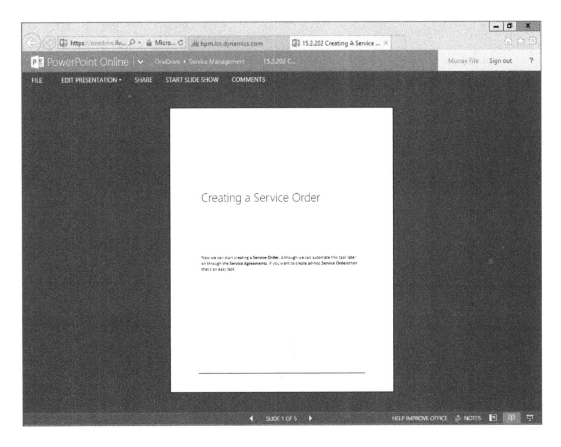

And now you can view the associated documentation ☺

Attach OneDrive Documents To Business Process Models Within Lifecycle Services

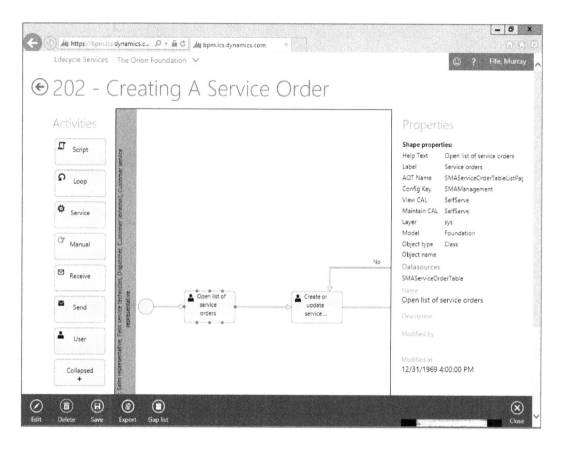

Additionally you can attach document links to steps within your business process models. To do this, open up your business process, select the step in the process that you want to attach documentation to and then click on the **Edit** button.

Attach OneDrive Documents To Business Process Models Within Lifecycle Services

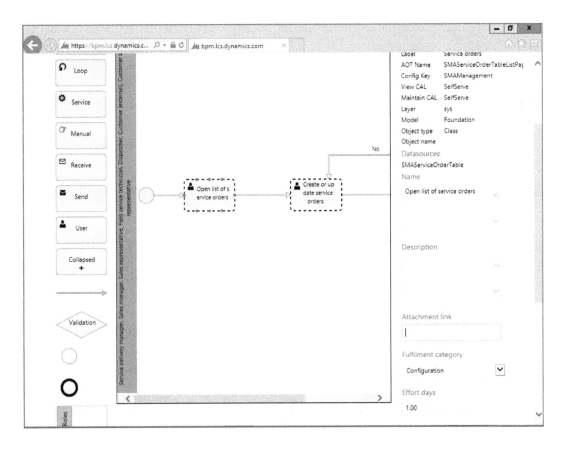

Within the properties pane you will see an option for the **Attachment Link**.

Attach OneDrive Documents To Business Process Models Within Lifecycle Services

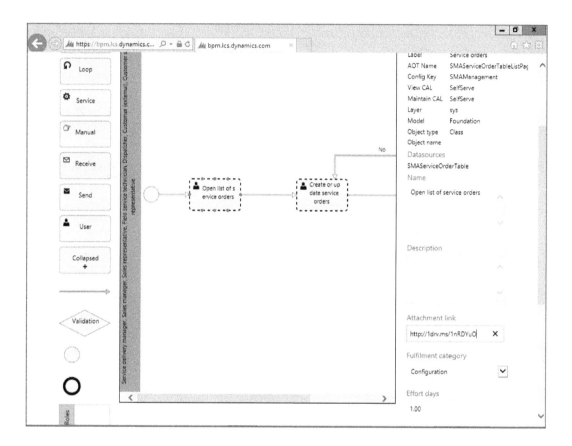

Just paste your URL into the **Attachment Link** field and save the step changes.

Attach OneDrive Documents To Business Process Models Within Lifecycle Services

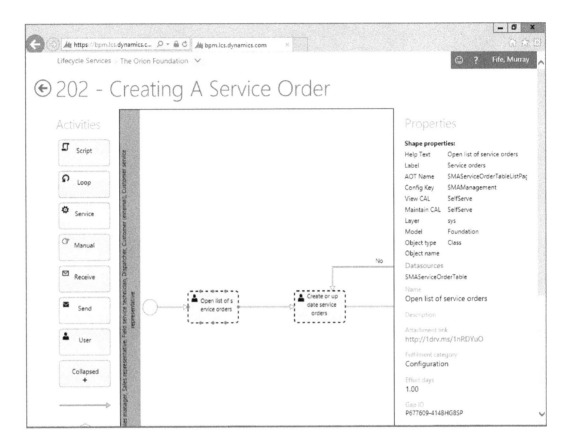

Now when you look at the properties pane, there is a link there that you can click that will take you straight to your OneDrive document.

How cool is that?

DEPLOYING DYNAMICS AX TEST SYSTEMS THROUGH AZURE

Azure is a great place to host your Dynamics AX environment, because it means that you don't have to invest in any hardware, servers, or high powered computers to run the test system. If you play your cards right, it may not even cost you a cent...

To make this even easier, Lifecycle Services offers a Cloud Hosted Environment tool that will create a Dynamics AX environment for you that is hosted through the Azure services within a couple of minutes – give and take 30 for the machine to be deployed. This is a great way to create a test system without requiring any investment in hardware, or software.

Signing Up For An Azure Account

The first step in this process is to make sure that you have an Azure account with Microsoft.

Signing Up For An Azure Account

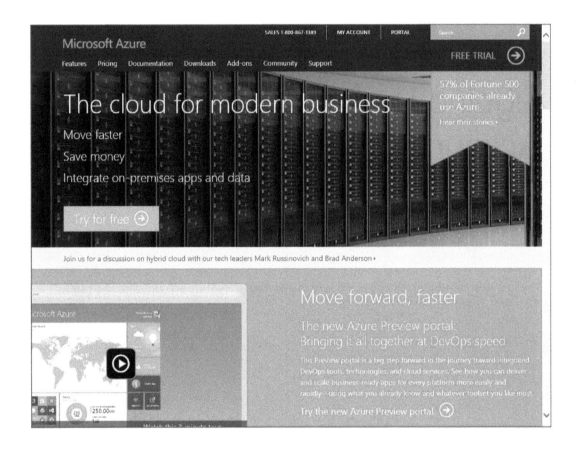

To do this just go to the Microsoft Azure site where you can sign up.

Signing Up For An Azure Account

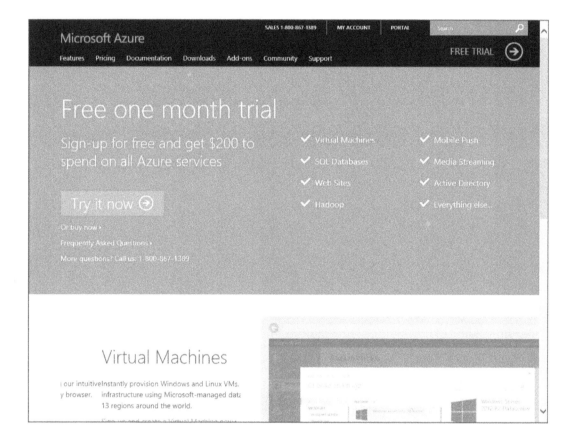

If you're lucky you may even be able to catch a promotion to test out the service.

Signing Up For An Azure Account

Also, if you have a MSDN account, then you may also get free credits towards your Azure account as well. This is what I use.

Once you have signed up, note down your **Subscription ID**.

Creating A Dynamics AX Instance On Azure Through Lifecycle Services

Once you have an Azure account, you can use Lifecycle Services to create a virtual test environment for you that is built off the standard demo system that Microsoft have built and populated with sample data.

Creating A Dynamics AX Instance On Azure Through Lifecycle Services

To do this, open up Lifecycle Services, and open up the project that you want to deploy the environment for. Then click on the **Cloud Hosted Environment** tile within the **Tools** group.

Creating A Dynamics AX Instance On Azure Through Lifecycle Services

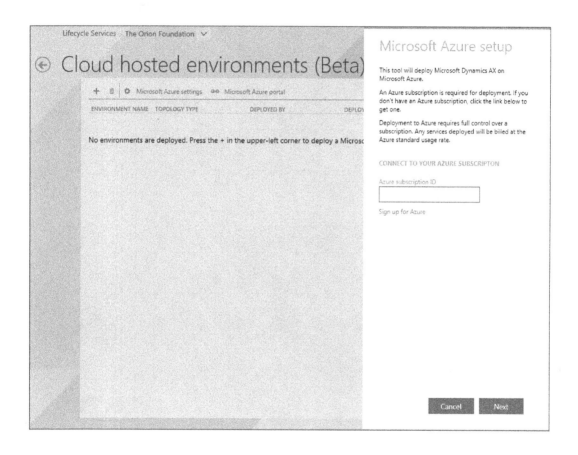

Lifecycle Services will then ask you to specify the Azure Subscription ID that you are using to host the virtual machine in.

Creating A Dynamics AX Instance On Azure Through Lifecycle Services

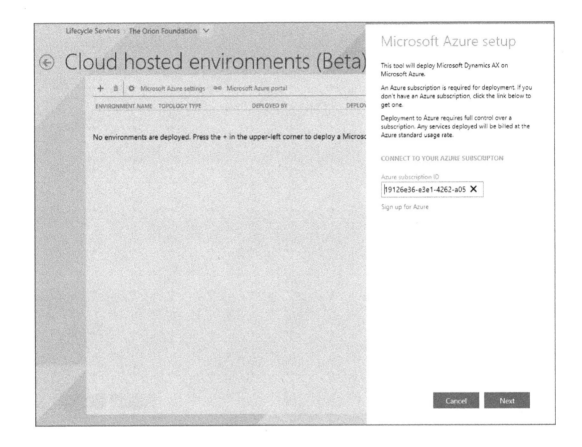

Return back to Lifecycle Services and paste in your **Azure Subscription ID** and click on the **Next** button.

Creating A Dynamics AX Instance On Azure Through Lifecycle Services

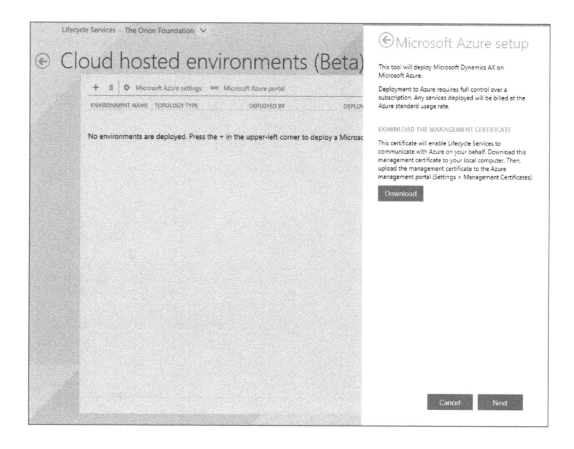

Then you will be asked to link Lifecycle Services with the Azure account. To do this, click the **Download** button to get your Management Certificate.

Creating A Dynamics AX Instance On Azure Through Lifecycle Services

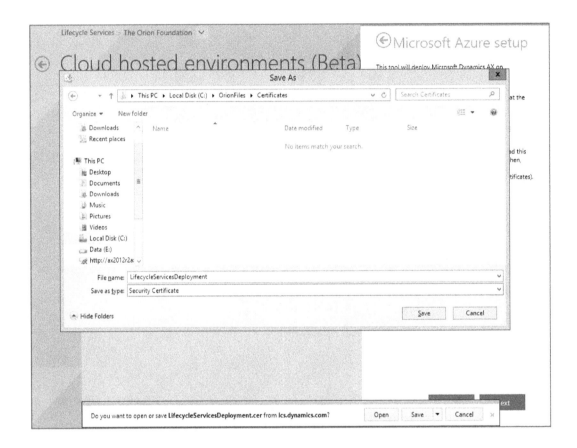

Then save the Certificate to your desktop.

Creating A Dynamics AX Instance On Azure Through Lifecycle Services

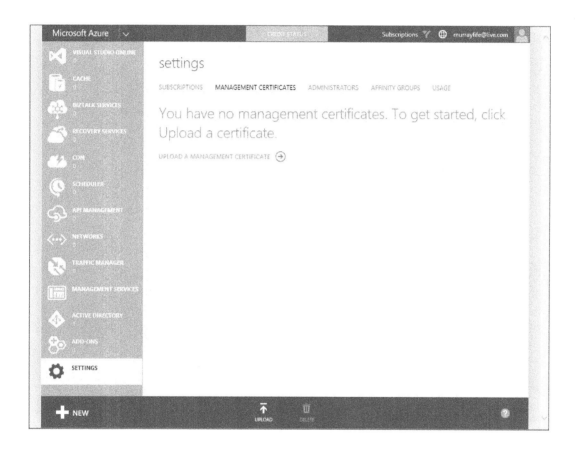

Return to Azure, and select the **Management Certificates** tab within the **Settings** group and then click on the **Upload** button in the bottom bar.

Creating A Dynamics AX Instance On Azure Through Lifecycle Services

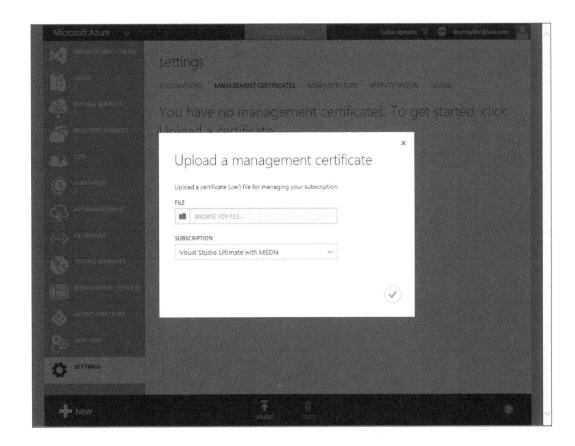

When the **Upload A Management Certificate** dialog is displayed, click on the **Browse For File** link.

Creating A Dynamics AX Instance On Azure Through Lifecycle Services

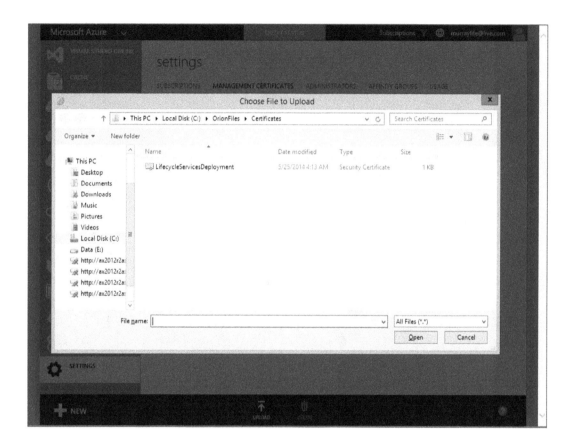

And then find the management certificate that you saved away and click the **Open** button.

Creating A Dynamics AX Instance On Azure Through Lifecycle Services

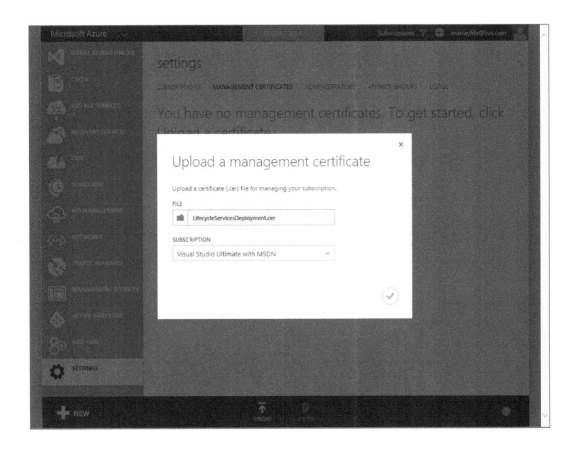

Then click the check box to upload the certificate.

Creating A Dynamics AX Instance On Azure Through Lifecycle Services

Now within Azure you should have a new **Management Certificate** record.

Creating A Dynamics AX Instance On Azure Through Lifecycle Services

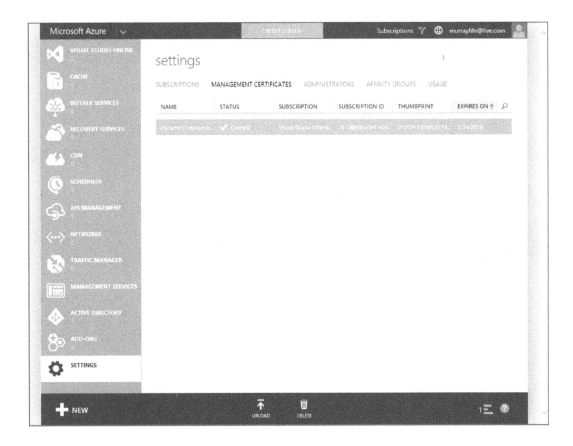

Note: it may take a minute for the certificate to upload.

Creating A Dynamics AX Instance On Azure Through Lifecycle Services

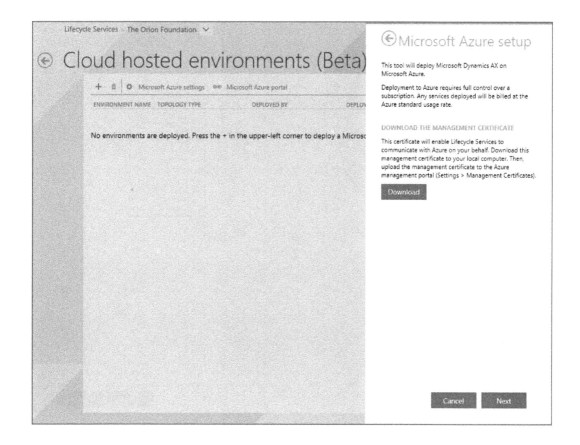

Now return to Lifecycle Services and click the **Next** button.

Creating A Dynamics AX Instance On Azure Through Lifecycle Services

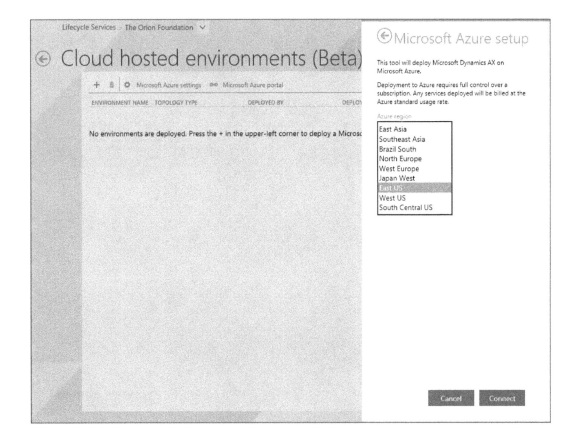

Specify your region, and then click the **Connect** button.

Creating A Dynamics AX Instance On Azure Through Lifecycle Services

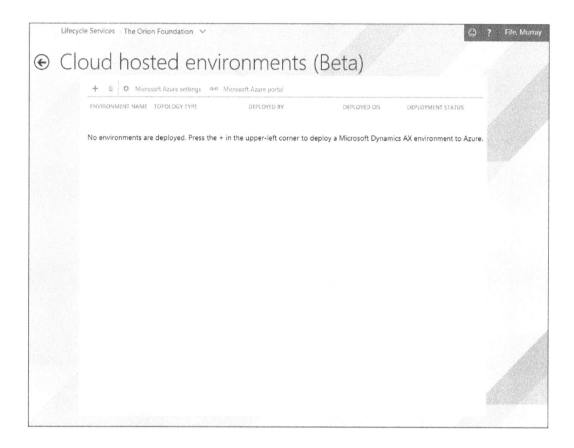

Now you will be able to access the **Cloud Hosted Environments** list form. To add a new demo server, click on the **+** icon in the top left of the form.

Creating A Dynamics AX Instance On Azure Through Lifecycle Services

You will then be given a list of possible environments.

Creating A Dynamics AX Instance On Azure Through Lifecycle Services

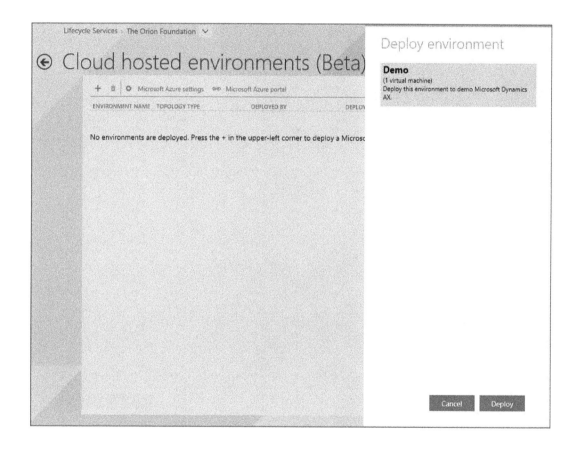

Select the version that you want to deploy and then click the **Deploy** button.

Creating A Dynamics AX Instance On Azure Through Lifecycle Services

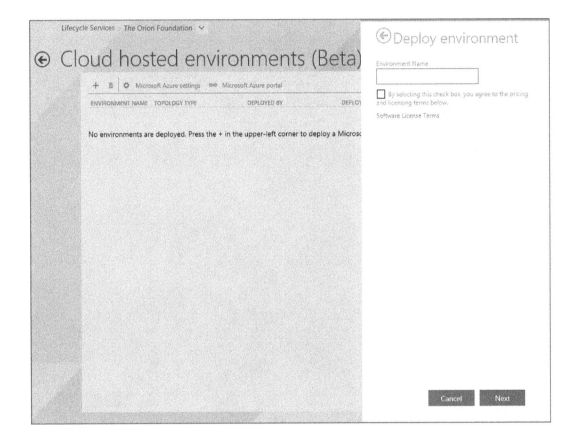

You will then be asked to set up your demo environment.

Creating A Dynamics AX Instance On Azure Through Lifecycle Services

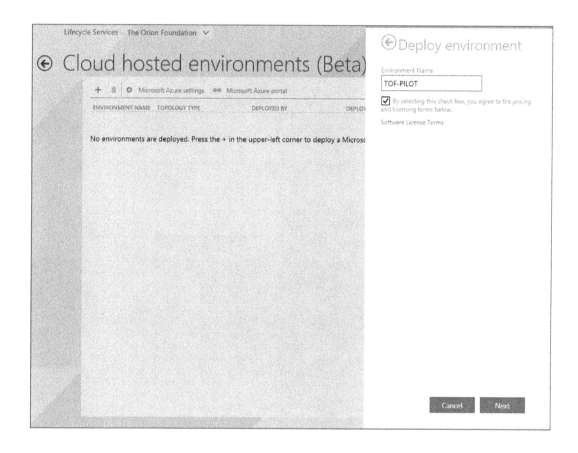

Give your environment a **Name**, check the mandatory agreement box, and then click the **Next** button.

Creating A Dynamics AX Instance On Azure Through Lifecycle Services

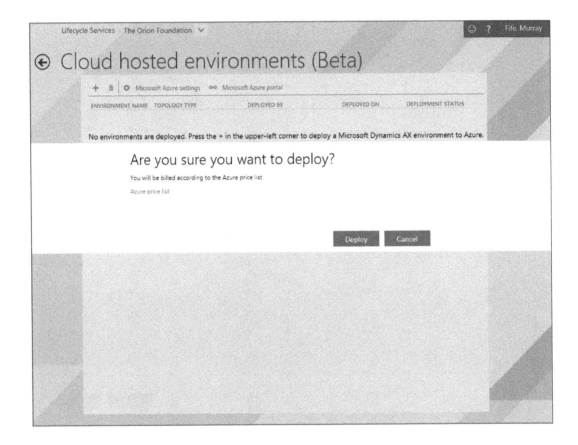

Finally, if you are sure that you want to do this, click the **Deploy** button.

Creating A Dynamics AX Instance On Azure Through Lifecycle Services

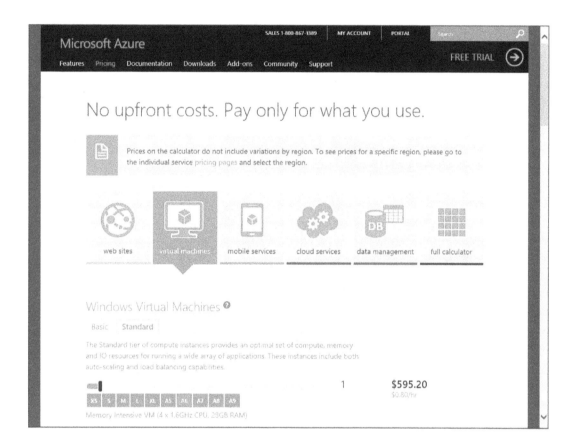

Disclaimer: If you run this particular version of the demo without turning it off then keep in mind that it will run you about $600 a month.

Creating A Dynamics AX Instance On Azure Through Lifecycle Services

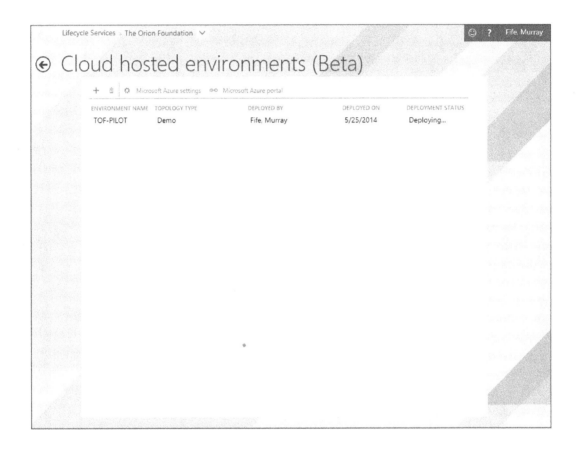

Now Azure needs to do a little bit of work to deploy the image. Now would be a good time to get a coffee – it will take 30 minutes or so.

Creating A Dynamics AX Instance On Azure Through Lifecycle Services

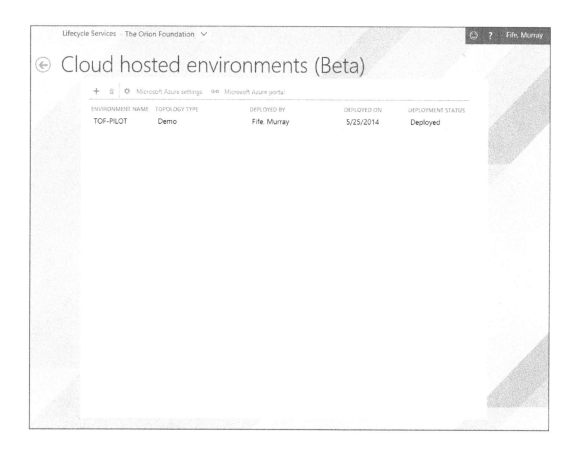

After a little bit, you will find that the image has been deployed.

Creating A Dynamics AX Instance On Azure Through Lifecycle Services

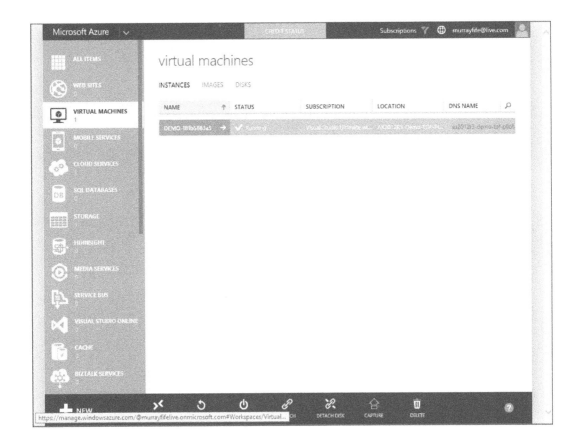

If you return to your Azure account you will notice that the server is now available. To access it just click on the **Connect** button in the footer of the form.

Creating A Dynamics AX Instance On Azure Through Lifecycle Services

And you will be able to log into the demo environment.

Creating A Dynamics AX Instance On Azure Through Lifecycle Services

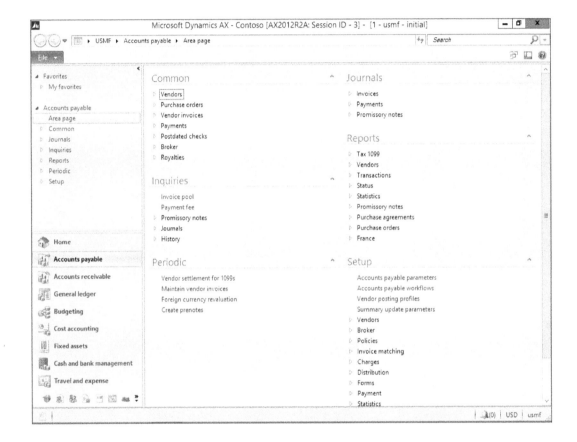

And Dynamics AX is already configured for you with the demo data.

That is super cool.

Creating A Dynamics AX Instance On Azure Through Lifecycle Services

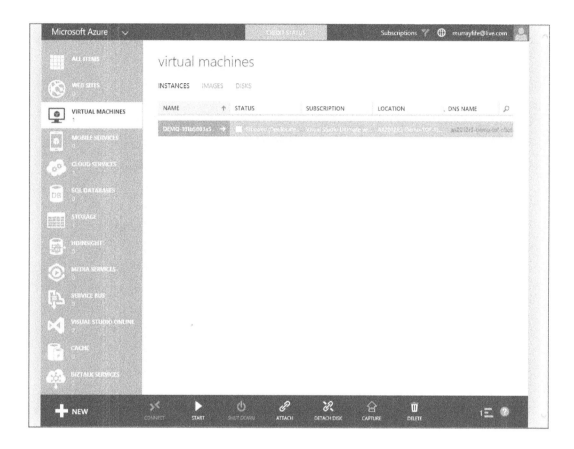

Tip: So that you don't get hit with a large bill at the end of the month, when you are not using the VM, just turn it off.

SUMMARY

Lifecycle Services is an incredibly important tool for any Dynamics AX project, because it gives everyone that is connected to the project access to all of the project information, and also gives you a way to link all of the business processes within Dynamics AX up to the project without a lot of extra work involved, making the project management side of the deployment so much simpler.

You would have to be fool not to take advantage of it.

About the Author

Murray Fife is a Microsoft Dynamics AX MVP, and Author with over 20 years of experience in the software industry.

Like most people in this industry he has paid his dues as a developer, an implementation consultant, a trainer, and now spend most of his days working with companies solving their problems with the Microsoft suite of products, specializing in the Dynamics® AX solutions.

EMAIL	murray@dynamicsaxcompanions.com
TWITTER	@murrayfife
SKYPE	murrayfife
AMAZON	www.amazon.com/author/murrayfife
WEB	www.dynamicsaxcompanions.com

www.ingramcontent.com/pod-product-compliance
Lightning Source LLC
Chambersburg PA
CBHW080152060326
40689CB00018B/3953